The PRIMARY SEND HANDBOOK for TRAINEE TEACHERS

The PRIMARY SEND HANDBOOK for TRAINEE TEACHERS

SARAH ALIX

1 Oliver's Yard
55 City Road
London EC1Y 1SP

2455 Teller Road
Thousand Oaks, California 91320

Unit No 323-333, Third Floor, F-Block
International Trade Tower Nehru Place
New Delhi – 110 019

8 Marina View Suite 43-053
Asia Square Tower 1
Singapore 018960

Editor: Delayna Spencer
Editorial Assistant: Harry Dixon
Production Editor: Gourav Kumar
Copyeditor: Clare Weaver
Indexer: KnowledgeWorks Global Ltd
Marketing Manager: Dilhara Attygalle
Cover Design: Wendy Scott
Typeset by KnowledgeWorks Global Ltd
Printed and bound by CPI Group (UK) Ltd, Croydon, CR0 4YY

Library of Congress Control Number: 2023947697

British Library Cataloguing in Publication data

A catalogue record for this book is available from the British Library

ISBN 978-1-5296-7269-5
ISBN 978-1-5296-7268-8 (pbk)

Contents

Author Biography

Dr Sarah Alix has worked in Education for 20 years. She works for the Sigma Trust in Essex leading the teacher training provision. Sarah has experience as a youth worker, a primary school teacher, a behaviour support advisor working with primary, secondary and special schools, and working for a University as a Senior Lecturer and Deputy Head of their Education Department.

Sarah has a Doctorate in Education, a psychology degree, and post-graduate qualifications including the SENCo award, PGCert in Autism, MA in Education, and PGCert in HE. Recent publications include researching autistic trainee teacher experiences, and a handbook for foster carers.

Sarah is also a Senior Fellow of the Higher Education Academy, a graduate member of the British Psychological Society and a Fellow of the Chartered College. She is part of the Autism Education Trust Expert Reference Group and Schools Reference Group.

Sarah has a great personal awareness and understanding of neurodiversity through her own family members who are autistic, have attention deficit hyperactivity disorder, dyslexia and general anxiety disorder, and through her own diagnosis of autism as an adult a few years ago.

Sarah has a strong belief that this is where it all starts: **education,** and that the school years lay the foundation for everything else to come, whether this is to work in health, finance, the arts, business or education to name a few, it all starts with the building blocks of school. This is why it is so important to promote the acceptance of differences, and to begin with this here within teacher training. Great teachers, with a secure understanding of how to adapt the curriculum for everyone, will make the difference to thousands of individuals each and every year.

Acknowledgements

After writing *The Neurodiversity Handbook for Trainee Teachers*, I thought it was really important to write a book such as this to support primary trainee teachers navigating the SEND system in school and understanding their role in this. The two books complement each other; this book outlining the SEND system, the role of the teacher, and giving an in-depth look at the four broad areas of need from the Code of Practice, and the neurodiversity handbook reflecting upon this within a neurodiversity framework. I would like to thank Sage Editor, Delayna Spencer for all of her support and guidance along the way with both books and to Ruth Lilly and Esme Sawyer for their support and guidance. I would also like to thank each of my children; Charlie, Morgan and Maximilian for being the unique individuals that they are. It is important to thank everyone that has supported and helped me to write this book, given me insight, and have had discussions with me to form the case studies. This includes experienced staff from the Sigma Trust, SENCos, learning mentors, Trainee Teachers, Early Career Teachers and Parents.

Introduction: How to use this Book

This book is a practical support book for primary Trainee Teachers, their mentors and teacher training tutors. It provides an overview of the Special Educational Needs and Disabilities (SEND) roles and responsibilities in schools, the broad areas of need, assessment and support for SEND pupils.

The chapters move through key areas to support SEND pupils, and there are three parts to this book:

1. *Part I* consists of Chapters One and Two in which the area of SEND is introduced, and the history of policy and legislation. How have we got to this point of supporting SEND pupils in schools? This section progresses to examine the roles and responsibilities of the SENCo and the class teacher in school in relation to supporting SEND pupils.
2. *Part II* focuses on the four broad areas of need that are outlined in the Code of Practice (CoP) (2015). There is a chapter dedicated to each of these four areas, in which the area is examined and consideration of how to support pupils with needs in each of these areas.
3. *Part III* looks at key areas of developing classroom practice in relation to SEND; relationships with other professionals, assessing pupil needs and there is a focus on Education, Health and Care Plans (EHC plans/ EHCPs).

There are links to the Core Content Framework and Teachers' Standards throughout.

The chapters draw upon expertise from Lead SENCos and SENCos in schools, and trainee and qualified teachers.

The book links directly to areas of the Core Content Framework, the Teachers' Standards and the SEND Code of Practice (CoP) (2015).

The book contains five types of interactive features throughout:

1. ***Reflect*** opportunities for the reader to reflect on areas of practice.
2. ***Professional Discussion*** for the reader to have with their class teacher, mentor, training tutor or SENCo.
3. ***Activity*** an opportunity to find something out or seek further information.
4. ***Strategies to Support Pupils*** outlining strategies for trainees to use (within Part II, Chapters 3 to 6).
5. ***Case Studies*** demonstrating examples of practice for reflection or discussion.

Key Documents Referenced throughout this Book

- *The Special Education Needs and Disabilities (SEND) Code of Practice (CoP) 2015:* This is a statutory code which contains the legal requirements for Local Authorities and schools, which outlines the roles and responsibilities that everyone has in relation to supporting pupils with SEND.
- *ITT Core Content Framework (CCF) 2019:* This is a document written by the Department for Education (DfE) that sets out the minimum entitlement of training for all trainee teachers. It outlines the knowledge, skills and behaviours that define teaching. Initial Teacher Training Providers include all of the areas outlined within the CCF, within their own teacher training curriculum. Each chapter of this book links to areas of the CCF, so that you can see which areas of your teacher training curriculum are covered within the section of the book, and these are outlined at the beginning of each chapter.
- *Teachers' Standards 2011:* these are the standards that you are assessed against at the end of your teacher training course and will determine if you pass the course and can progress to become an Early Career Teacher (ECT). You are required to meet these standards consistently throughout your teaching career. Each chapter links to areas of the Teachers' Standards, and these are outlined towards the end of each chapter so that you can connect the area that you have been working on and progressing towards meeting the standards.
- *Initial Teacher Training and Early Career Framework:* This is a new document written by the Department for Education (DfE) (published January 2024) which is set to replace the CCF and ECF (September 2025). At the time of writing, this is not in use yet. The content is very similar to the CCF with a few more references to adaptive teaching and SEND, which are already covered within this book.

Part I

Policy and Teacher Responsibilities

1

Policy Development and Legislation in the UK Context

Chapter Aims

- To understand how policy and legislation relating to SEND has changed over time.
- To consider what policy and legislation looks like in schools today.
- To understand the Local Authority's role in providing provision for SEND pupils.
- To gain an overview of the meaning of inclusion and different settings for SEND pupils.
- To gain an initial understanding of intersectionality, and how this may impact pupils in class.
- To have an overview of the categories of complex needs.
- To understand the importance of the Code of Practice (CoP) in school and how this informs the following chapters.
- To begin to understand how policy is changing, and what this might mean for class teachers.

Links to the Core Content Framework (CCF)

High Expectations

- ***Learn that*** a culture of mutual trust and respect supports effective relationships.
- ***Learn how to*** use intentional and consistent language that promotes challenge and aspiration.

Adaptive Teaching

- ***Learn that*** seeking to understand pupils' differences, including their different levels of prior knowledge and potential barriers to learning, is an essential part of teaching.

Professional Behaviours

- ***Learn that*** reflective practice, supported by feedback from, and observation of experienced colleagues, professional debate, and learning from educational research, is also likely to support improvement.
- ***Learn that*** SENCos, pastoral leaders, careers advisors and other specialist colleagues also have valuable expertise and can ensure that appropriate support is in place for pupils.
- ***Learn how to*** engage critically with research and use evidence to critique practice.

Introduction

Consideration of SEND pupils in schools has changed and developed dramatically over the decades. This chapter will look at these developments so that you can understand how we have arrived at the system that is currently in place in schools, and you can consider why we have the systems and processes that we do, what challenges current systems pose to class teachers, and how you might implement current policy and legislation in your own classroom.

So, what is a Special Educational Need or Disability in this context?

Reflect

What is your current understanding of the term 'Special Educational Need or Disability' within schools?

Definitions of SEND

A child has a Special Educational Need or Disability if they have a learning difficulty or disability which means that they need to have a different or additional provision made for them. The DfE (2015) outline this as:

- has a significantly greater difficulty in learning than the majority of others of the same age, or
- has a disability which prevents or hinders him or her from making use of facilities of a kind generally provided for others of the same age in mainstream schools or mainstream post-16 institutions.

(DfE, 2015)

The Equality Act 2010 outlines that a child who has SEN may have a disability if they have a 'physical or mental impairment which has a long-term and substantial adverse effect on their ability to carry out normal day-to-day activities'. Many children could be included within this definition and long-term is referred to as a year or more, and substantial as being more than minor. Incorporated within this are children with impairments such as a sight or hearing loss, and long-term health conditions such as diabetes, epilepsy and asthma. Children with conditions such as these do not necessarily have SEN, but there can be a significant overlap between children with conditions such as these and those with SEN.

Key Policy Development and Legislation in the UK

The Department for Education (DfE) (2015) set out their vision in the Code of Practice (COP) (discussed in detail later in the chapter) for pupils with Special Educational Needs and Disabilities (SEND); the vision 'is the same as for all children and young people – that they achieve well in their early years, at school and in college, and lead happy and fulfilled lives'.

So, how did we get to this point, what did that journey look like, and where are we heading to? Table 1.1 outlines key policy and legislation in relation to SEND and also key developments in teacher training relating to SEND.

You will see the first defining moment related to the Education Act in 1944, in which pupils were categorised and placed within special schools. *The Neurodiversity Handbook for Trainee Teachers* outlines a different approach to a medical model and shifts thinking towards a model of difference rather than deficit. The reference can be found in the further reading section of the chapter.

The key document outlining the duties of the school, SENCo and teachers is the Code of Practice (2014/15). This document has defined practice for nearly the last decade. However, change is on the horizon with the SEND and Alternative Provision (AP) Improvement Plan released in 2023. This dovetails with the Schools' white paper (2023)

Table 1.1 Timeline of Significant Policy and Legislation relating to SEND.

Year	Policy or Legislation	Outline/Comments
1944	Education Act 1944	Children with SEND were categorised by disability which was defined in medical terms. They were considered as 'uneducable' 'maladjusted' or 'educationally sub-normal' and in need of special educational 'treatment' within a special school. We have moved on from this thinking in many ways, but there is still some way to go. A good text to read on this is *The Neurodiversity Handbook for Trainee Teachers*, Alix, S. (2023).
1978	The Warnock Report	Baroness Warnock introduced a radical idea of 'statements' to support an integrative approach which later became known as 'inclusion'.
1981	Education Act 1981	The term 'Special Educational Needs' was introduced, and there was a greater emphasis on integrated provision.
1990s		The Warnock framework became embedded in schools.
1994		The SENCO role was established in England.
1997	Green paper; Excellence for All	This paper adopted the principle of inclusion as an extension of the capacity of mainstream schools.
2001	Special Educational Needs and Disabilities Act 2001 (SENDA)	This covered disabled people's rights within the provision of education.
2004	Special Educational Needs and Disabilities; Towards Inclusive Schools. Ofsted report	This report looked at how prepared mainstream schools were in supporting SEND pupils.
2010	The Equality Act 2010	This act consolidated acts in relation to discrimination.
2011	Teachers' Standards	A set of standards outlining the minimum requirements for teachers' practice and conduct.
2014	The Children and Families Act 2014	A commitment to improve services for all children regardless of their background. It outlined specific duties on schools to support all children with SEN.
2014	SEND Code of Practice	Outlined the duties for SEND in schools under the new law.
2015	The Carter Review of Initial Teacher Training	This review highlighted areas of good practice and areas to be improved on. Training for trainee teachers on SEND was included as a recommendation (1g).
2015	SEND Code of Practice updates	Revisions were made to the Code of Practice, and is the version that is currently in place today.
2016		Basic SEND training became compulsory for Trainee Teachers following recommendations from the Carter review of Initial Teacher Training (ITT).
2019	The Core Content Framework	This document defines the minimum entitlement regarding the training of trainee teachers.
2022	SEND review green paper	This paper acknowledged that change was needed using the phrase 'right support, right place, right time'.
2023	SEND and Alternative Provision (AP) Improvement Plan	The improvement plan sets out the next steps for SEND provision in schools – the link to this document is in the further reading section of the chapter.

and will impact upon your own practice as a developing trainee teacher, and as a qualified teacher. This area will be outlined towards the end of this chapter and examined closely in the conclusions chapter of this book.

Expectations of the Local Authority

The Local Authority (LA) has a key role and legal responsibilities in providing support and provision for pupils with SEND. They have a legal duty to identify and assess the special educational needs of pupils that they are responsible for. The LA becomes responsible for a child when they become aware that a pupil may have or has SEND.

First, the child's setting (nursery, school, post-16 provision) has a responsibility to support a pupil with SEND. However, if the setting believes that a pupil needs more support than the setting can give them, then a referral is made to the LA for an Education, Health and Care Needs Assessment (EHCNA). This assessment could then lead to an Education, Health and Care Plan (EHCP or EHC plan) which are discussed in detail in Chapter 9. The EHC plan will set out the additional support that the pupil needs. Once this provision has been specified in an EHC plan, it is a legal document, and the LA has a legal duty to ensure that this provision is provided to the pupil.

The LA must publish something called the 'Local Offer', which is found on their website and contains a list of all the services and support that they expect pupils and families with SEND will be able to draw upon for support. It will include all the services that are available within their geographical area of the LA, and also services outside their own LA that pupils are able to access. It might include services such as therapy, care placements or independent schools. This list should not just be a list of links, but will provide details on what settings will provide from the SEND funding, what training provision will include, what transport arrangements will be provided and what support will be provided for adulthood and independent living. It is important to note that the Local Offer is not legally binding, and there is no guarantee that something listed in the offer will be available.

Inclusion and Different Settings for SEND Pupils (outside a mainstream setting)

All schools have a responsibility to provide appropriate support to pupils with SEND. Some pupils will need further specialist support beyond what a mainstream school can provide. Every school must have a designated teacher for co-ordinating the SEND provision, and this is the SENCo. Further guidance on the role and responsibilities of the SENCo are outlined in Chapter 2. The SENCo must inform parents when special educational provision is put in place for a pupil.

Pupils in a mainstream school with SEND must be able to access activities and a 'broad and balanced curriculum' (CoP, 2015) alongside their peers without SEND, and it is the responsibility of the school to ensure that arrangements are in place for this access. SEND pupils should be able to access a full range of the curriculum subjects and content, and reasonable adjustments made to support pupils to access this. These adjustments will be explored further in Chapters 3 to 6.

A member of the school's governing body should be assigned to having a specific oversight of the school's provision for SEND pupils, and school leaders and the governing body should review this provision regularly.

This book will focus on what SEND in mainstream schools will look like as this is where you, as a trainee teacher, will have the majority, or all of your placements and training. However, the book will draw upon experiences and practice from alternative settings, and guidance such as the Code of Practice is applicable across all settings.

Special schools

Approximately 2 per cent of pupils attend a special school, with the majority having an EHCP. Special schools provide education for pupils with a special educational need or disability. They are a type of school that caters for pupils who cannot access education in a mainstream setting because of their learning difficulty or disability, and whose parents or carers have requested a special school placement and the Local Authority has agreed to arranging this place. Special schools can be a maintained school, an academy or an independent school. The age ranges of pupils vary in special schools, some educate pupils from the age of three to nineteen (and even up to twenty-five), with others focusing on primary or secondary age phases.

Some special schools will support pupils with a broad range of needs, and others will focus around a category as outlined in the CoP and listed in the section on the CoP later in this chapter. Some schools will focus on autism, or speech and language needs, or have a hub or base within a school for these areas. Mainstream schools may also have a base such as this within their school.

Special schools have a higher staff to pupil ratio than mainstream schools and class sizes are normally smaller, with teachers and teaching assistants likely to have more specialist training in SEND. They will also have access to and provide a range of services and interventions which will include a speech and language therapist (who may be trained in the use of Picture Exchange Communication Systems (PECS) or Makaton), physiotherapist, and a school nurse. Many special schools will also have specialist equipment and rooms that mainstream schools do not have, such as a therapy pool, sensory rooms, and adapted outdoor play equipment or gym equipment.

Positives of a special school are:

- higher staff to pupil ratio with smaller class sizes;
- specialist trained teachers;
- pupils mix with peers with similar needs and challenges, which supports positive self-esteem and reduces bullying;

- specialist therapists;
- specialist resources.

There can also be some drawbacks:

- The school may offer a limited curriculum and fewer qualifications or GCSEs.
- Pupils may need to travel a longer distance from home.
- The lack of opportunity for pupils to socialise with a range of peers of their own age or from their home area if they travel to school.

Alternative provision

An alternative provision arrangement can be made for a pupil when they would not otherwise receive a suitable education based upon their age, aptitude and any SEN they may have. The education arrangements made must be full-time, unless it is deemed that it is in the best interests of the child that a reduced timetable or level of education should be in place, and should only be seen as a temporary measure. The alternative provision should be made in line with their EHCP.

CASE STUDY

Lexi attended a mainstream primary school and was in Year 4. Lexi was having difficulty regulating her emotions around previous trauma, and this was evident in her increasing challenges with behaviour and being able to regulate within a busy classroom environment. There was on-going support with a range of therapies, but knowing that this would take time to demonstrate an impact, the school and parents decided it would be better for Lexi to spend time in a smaller provision in a quieter and calmer environment. The school had an on-site facility named 'grow' for pupils such as Lexi that needed additional support, with the intention that this was a short-term provision and that Lexi would return to mainstream school again in approximately half a term to a term. The provision supported pupils from a number of schools in the local area. A referral was made into the provision and a space was secured for Lexi. Lexi spent a term at the provision and was supported with recognising her emotions and using strategies to support her own regulation of emotions so that her behaviour did not escalate as quickly and as extreme as it had previously. This was supported through one-to-one interventions, and therapy from outside agencies including mental health support. Lexi then reintegrated back into the mainstream class within Year 5 with continued support.

When this education is based anywhere other than a school, it is known as an alternative provision. It could include a Pupil Referral Unit (PRU), alternative provision academy or alternative provision free school. Alternative provision may be suitable for a pupil that has barriers to learning associated with a school setting.

Pupil Referral Units (PRUs)

PRUs are for pupils that face barriers within a mainstream school. The LA funds PRUs and it is their responsibility to provide a full-time education to all children. A PRU is an alternative way from mainstream school of doing this. Pupils that attend PRUs are often referred there as they need greater care and support than their mainstream school can provide for them. This will include pupils that:

- experience Social, Emotional and Mental Health (SEMH) needs;
- have behavioural challenges relating to SEMH needs;
- refuse to attend school;
- are permanently excluded from school or are at risk of permanent exclusion;
- have specific SEND which can be supported better within a PRU;
- are a new school starter who had missed out on a school place;
- are a pregnant or young mother.

Some pupils will have all of their lessons at the PRU, while others will spend part of the time at the PRU and part of the time at a mainstream school. PRUs are not special schools and cannot provide the same level of education for pupils with SEND, so this should not be seen as a long-term educational setting for them. PRUs can be a challenging but rewarding place to work as part of your career, and it may be a setting to gain some experience in as part of your teacher training.

PROFESSIONAL **DISCUSSION**

Discuss with your teacher training provider whether there is the opportunity to spend a day or two in a PRU or at an alternative provision as part of your course. Some courses will include this as part of the course, others are happy to arrange an experience such as this for you. It is better to go towards the middle or end of your course when you can reflect on what you have learnt so far, and how this transfers to an alternative provision.

Elective Home Education (EHE)

Any pupil including those with SEND can be educated at home if parents choose to do this. A parent would notify the school this is what they are going to do, and the pupil would be removed from the school register.

Children could be electively home educated from the age of five, and may never attend a school setting, or they may be removed from school and taken off roll to be home educated. Home education can work well when regard for the needs of the child have been considered and it is appropriate and well-delivered. Parents may choose EHE because a child is struggling in a school environment, they may have extreme levels of anxiety, have sensory needs or they may be at risk of exclusion.

If a child has been withdrawn from a child for EHE then the school do not need to provide any support. The LA can provide discretionary support, including support for SEND, and once a child is home educated, the LA will look into the suitability of the education being provided for the child. If the education being provided is not deemed as suitable, then a School Attendance Order, or Education Supervision Order can be applied for by the LA to the court.

It is important to note that parents should not be asked by a school to EHE their child. This is something called 'off-rolling' when a child is purposefully taken off a school register, and when this is in the best interest of a school, and not in the best interest of a child, for example, in order to make a school look more positive for example with data or exam results.

Intersectionality

Intersectionality is the interconnection of social categories such as class, ethnicity, gender identity, gender expression, race and religious beliefs, and how they overlap and are applied to an individual in the form of discrimination or disadvantage. It is a way of describing how multiple forms of inequality combine and compound to form an obstacle.

By understanding intersectionality further, we can gain an understanding of the individual differences we all have, the challenges we face, and the impact of the connection of these categories on us. Within education, it is important to understand the impact of intersectionality, and how we, as educationalists, may miss an opportunity to support a pupil because of our assumptions towards the challenges within a particular category, and miss other underlying factors. For example, Waitoller and Kozleski (2013) describe how a refugee pupil with behavioural challenges is excluded because the school fails to address their identity and instead only supports one area of need. The school supports and provides services in relation to their disability, but fails to support sufficiently with learning language and with the trauma the pupil has experienced.

By understanding and considering intersectionality for our pupils, we can understand the difference between us and the complexities that individual pupils may encounter. Intersectionality will be interwoven into the chapters of the book and you should consider the potential impact and challenges when considering pupils, or looking at the case studies.

Complex Needs

Severe Learning Difficulty or Disability (SLD)

Pupils with SLD have significant cognitive difficulties. They will have difficulty accessing and participating in the school curriculum and will need carefully adjusted support for their needs. They may also have mobility and coordination difficulties, and challenges with communication, independence and social skills. Some pupils may have difficulty using speech and language, some will be able to hold simple conversations, others may use signs and symbols such as Makaton, or a picture exchange system.

Profound and Multiple Learning Difficulty (PMLD)

Pupils with PMLD have complex learning needs. They will have severe learning difficulties, combined with physical disabilities, possible medical conditions and sensory challenges. Pupils with PMLD will need a high level of support from adults for learning needs and for personal everyday care. The curriculum is likely to consist of sensory stimulation and small steps. Verbal communication will be limited, and include gestures, pointing, simple language and through support systems.

Complex Learning Difficulties or Disabilities (CLDD)

Pupils with CLDD have co-existing conditions and difficulties. These conditions overlap and therefore create a complex profile of needs. These pupils will have challenges in areas of mental health, relationships, behaviour, medical, physical, sensory, communication and cognitive. Progress in the curriculum may be inconsistent for these pupils.

The Code of Practice; the Developing Landscape

The Code of Practice (CoP) is statutory guidance for organisations such as schools and nurseries that support children with special educational needs and disabilities. It applies to maintained schools, academies and free schools. Although it is guidance, and not a legal document in itself, it does contain legal requirements and statutory guidelines as set out in the Children and Families Act 2014, the Equality Act 2010, and the Special Educational Needs and Disability Regulations 2014. The CoP includes details of legal requirements that must be followed without exception, and statutory guidance that must be followed by law unless there is a good reason not to. The CoP ensures that everyone, such as schools, governors, SENCos and Local Authorities are aware of their legal obligations and they can be held to account if they are not followed.

The CoP is set out to ensure that there is a consistent approach across the country, and that all pupils with SEND are given the same approach and care and therefore reduces the chance of a postcode lottery.

So, what does the CoP mean directly for schools? It states that all children and young people are entitled to an appropriate education, and that 'every school is required to identify and address the SEN of the pupils that they support' (CoP, 2015).

It includes the following:

- Ensuring that children and young people with SEND engage in the activities of the school alongside pupils who do not have SEND.
- Designating a teacher to be responsible for co-ordinating SEND provision – the SEND co-ordinator, or SENCo.
- Informing parents when they are making special educational provision for a child.
- Preparing a SEND information report that contains their arrangements for the admission of disabled children; the steps being taken to prevent disabled children from being treated less favourably than others; the facilities provided to enable access to the school for disabled children; and their accessibility plan that illustrates how they plan to improve access progressively over time.
- SEND children should also be identified on a SEND Register with provision mapping in place.
- Training must be delivered to help staff identify and support children with SEND to ensure early identification.

The CoP outlines areas of needs that pupils with SEND have.

The four broad areas of need that are outlined in the COP are discussed in detail in Part II of the book; Chapters 3 to 6. They are:

- Communication and interaction.
- Cognition and learning.
- Social, emotional and mental health difficulties.
- Sensory and/or physical needs.

The SEND and Alternative Provision (AP) Improvement Plan

Initially, a green paper was published as part of a sixteen-week consultation around SEND provision in schools. From this, the SEND and AP Improvement Plan (2023) was created and published. It sets out the government's proposals to improve outcomes for pupils through:

- improving experiences for families, reducing the current adversity and frustration that they face;
- delivering financial sustainability of the system;
- relieving pressure on the current AP sector.

They are aiming to deliver this through their mission:

- Fulfil children's potential: children and young people with SEND (or attending alternative provision) enjoy their childhood, achieve good outcomes and are well prepared for adulthood and employment.

- Build parents' trust: parents and carers experience a fairer, easily navigable system (across education, health and care) that restores their confidence that their children will get the right support, in the right place, at the right time.
- Provide financial sustainability: local leaders make the best use of record investment in the high needs budget to meet children and young people's needs and improve outcomes, while placing local authorities on a stable financial footing.

DfE (2023)

The DfE have a clear vision on what they would like to achieve; however, at the moment, as this is in the first stage of implementation, there will be challenges and discussions ahead from organisations such as the Local Government Association, and from schools, SENCos and families, on how this will be implemented. As you progress through the next few years of your early career, it is important to keep up to date with the progress and challenges ahead, and what this will mean for you as a practitioner in the classroom.

So, what do you need to know? First, there are no imminent changes to legislation, so assessment needs stay the same and applications for EHC plans. However, there is a clear direction that overall the DfE would like to reduce the number of EHC plans through secure provision in place and a well-functioning system across mainstream schools without the need for everyone currently with an EHCP to have one. This change will be slow moving though.

Some of the areas that the plan needs to address will be as follows:

- To ensure that in practice it improves the education support for pupils with SEND and their families.
- That Local Authorities are able to comply with the legal duties through having the resourcing and funding that they need.
- To ensure that training in SEND is available so that every teacher can be a teacher of their pupils with SEND.
- Support continues so that young people gain the support that they need to thrive as adults.
- Early support is given for families with pupils under five years old with emerging SEND.

What will happen first?

- The development of the National Standards, with input from LAs, health, professionals, practitioners, parents, carers and young people.
- Once these have been decided, then the testing of some of the elements of the standards with some regional partnerships.
- The establishing of a steering group to oversee the work being carried out within the plan.
- The creation and publication of a dashboard to support the implementation and the development of the local inclusion plans.

There is a SEND and AP roadmap, with projected timelines for change and implementation, the link to this is in the further reading section of the chapter. As you will see, there is a lot of change to take place, which will take some time and review if it is to make the progress and achieve the vision that is set out.

Activity

Research what changes are happening in SEND at the current time.

- Where on the SEND and AP roadmap have we reached?
- How might this impact you as you move into your teacher training year?
- What might you need to be aware of as you read through this book?

Recent Developments

As we know from earlier in the chapter, there has been a green paper review of SEND which has led to the SEND and Alternative Provision (AP) Improvement Plan. There are many changes to come over the next few years, and as we progress through the book, there will be reference to the current system in place, and the proposed changes and developments. Schools take time to change and embed practice; it can take several years for changes to be fully embedded and embraced by staff and systems. It is therefore important to have a whole picture within this book so that you can gain an understanding of the journey schools are going on in relation to SEND practice, and that when you enter a school, it might be in a different place to another school that you have visited or had a school placement with.

PROFESSIONAL DISCUSSION

Discuss with your mentor and/or school SENCo:

- What recent changes have been happening in your school in relation to SEND?
- What is working well?
- What is the next step in developments for the school?
- How does this link with the findings that you have read about in the previous activity?

Chapter Summary

This chapter began by looking at the definition of SEND and beginning to understand what SEND is. The chapters will go into further depth around the areas of SEND as we progress through the book. Key policy developments were outlined, which brings us up to date with the SEND landscape as we see it today, and the expectations and responsibilities of the Local Authority were outlined.

An overview of the different settings for SEND pupils outside of mainstream settings was introduced, and the terminology relating to complex needs. There was a section explaining intersectionality which will be woven throughout the book.

The final sections explained what the Code of Practice is and this will be explored further as we unpack the areas of SEND, and there was a forward look at the SEND and AP Improvement Plan.

Glossary of Key Terms

- Alternative Provision (AP) – education that is based anywhere other than a school.
- Code of Practice (CoP) – statutory guidance to support pupils with SEND.
- Education, Health and Care Plan (EHCP) – a legal document containing the provision that is set out for a pupil with SEND.
- Intersectionality – the interconnection of social categories, for example, class, ethnicity and gender, and the overlapping system of discrimination or disadvantage.
- Local Offer – the services and support that a Local Authority lists for potential access by families and schools for pupils with SEND.

Further Reading

- Alix, S. (2023). *The Neurodiversity Handbook for Trainee Teachers*. London: Sage.
- Department for Education (DfE) (2015). Special Educational Needs and Disabilities Code of Practice; 0 to 25 Years. DfE. https://assets.publishing.service.gov.uk/government/uploads/system/uploads/attachment_data/file/398815/SEND_Code_of_Practice_January_2015.pdf
- Department for Education (DfE) (2023). SEND and Alternative Provision Improvement Plan. https://www.gov.uk/government/publications/send-and-alternative-provision-improvement-plan
- Department for Education (DfE) (2023). SEND and Alternative Provision Improvement Plan Roadmap. https://www.gov.uk/government/publications/send-and-alternative-provision-improvement-plan/send-and-alternative-provision-roadmap
- Devarakonda, Chandrika (2022). SEND: Looking Through an Intersectionality Lens. https://www.bera.ac.uk/blog/send-looking-through-an-intersectionality-lens
- Independent Provider of Special Education Advice (IPSEA). https://www.ipsea.org.uk/

- Local Government Association. https://www.local.gov.uk/parliament/briefings-and-responses/send-and-alternative-provision-improvement-plan-2-march-2023

Links to the Teachers' Standards

- *1. Set high expectations which inspire, motivate and challenge pupils*; establish a safe and stimulating environment for pupils, rooted in mutual respect.
- *5. Adapt teaching to respond to the strengths and needs of all pupils;* have a secure understanding of how a range of factors can inhibit pupils' ability to learn, and how best to overcome these.

Part Two: Personal and Professional Conduct

- 3. Teachers must have an understanding of, and always act within, the statutory frameworks which set out their professional duties and responsibilities.

References

Alix, S. (2023). *The Neurodiversity Handbook for Trainee Teachers*. London: Sage.

Department for Education (DfE) (2015). Special Educational Needs and Disabilities Code of Practice; 0 to 25 Years. DfE.

UK Government (2010). The Equality Act 2010. https://www.legislation.gov.uk/ukpga/2010/15/contents

Waitoller, F. and Kozleski, E. B. (2013). Understanding and dismantling barriers for partnerships for inclusive education: A cultural historical activity theory perspective. *International Journal of Whole Schooling*, 23–42.

2

The Role of the SENCo, Class Teacher and their Responsibilities

Chapter Aims

- To understand the role of the SENCo.
- To know the responsibilities that the SENCo has.
- To understand the responsibilities that a class teacher has and how they are supported in these responsibilities by the SENCo.
- To begin to understand the challenges of teaching a class with a high number of SEND pupils in.

Links to the Core Content Framework (CCF)

High Expectations

- ***Learn that*** a culture of mutual trust and respect supports effective relationships.
- ***Learn that*** teachers are key role models, who can influence the attitudes, values and behaviours of their pupils.

Adaptive Teaching

- ***Learn how to*** receive clear, consistent and effective mentoring in supporting pupils with a range of additional needs, including how to use the SEND Code of Practice, which provides additional guidance on supporting pupils with SEND effectively.

Professional Behaviours

- ***Learn that*** effective professional development is likely to be sustained over time, involve expert support or coaching and opportunities for collaboration.
- ***Learn that*** reflective practice, supported by feedback from, and observation of experienced colleagues, professional debate, and learning from educational research, is also likely to support improvement.
- ***Learn that*** SENCos, pastoral leaders, careers advisors and other specialist colleagues also have valuable expertise and can ensure that appropriate support is in place for pupils.

Introduction

This chapter is going to have an in-depth look at the roles and responsibilities of key staff in school – the SENCo, your position as a class teacher – and how they work together.

The Roles and Responsibilities of the SENCo

It is required by law for every school to have a SENCo. They must be a qualified teacher, with Qualified Teacher Status (QTS), or be actively working towards becoming a qualified teacher, with the likelihood to become one in the near future. The Special Education Needs Code of Practice (CoP), as discussed in Chapter 1, requires that all SENCos must gain the National SENCo Award within three years of taking on the role of a SENCo. This award is offered by some universities as a Post-Graduate Certificate (PGCert) leading to the NASENCo Award, and there is now the new National Professional Qualification (NPQ) in being a SENCo. There are pros and cons of each route in relation to workload, the qualification itself and possibly carrying credits forward, for example towards a Master's, and the practical aspects of the qualifications. Although you are at the beginning stage of your teaching career and your teacher training, you may, at some stage in the next five years or more, consider becoming a SENCo yourself if you have an interest in working more strategically with pupils with SEND, and many of you will want to take this as a career progression route. It will therefore be important to have a good understanding of the role, and how it will develop and change, and the qualifications involved in pursuing this as your career. Most SENCos will be carrying out this qualification alongside their SENCo duties, and assignments will relate to their work, such as, analysing a case study, or developing their improvement plan.

The SENCo role is critical in ensuring that pupils with SEND receive the support that they need within the classroom and the wider school environment. The role has grown in importance over the last decade, and rightly so. The CoP outlines that the SENCo must be a qualified teacher and achieve the National SENCo Award, whereas previously, this was not the case.

The SENCo also has a key role in working with the Headteacher and the Governing body of the school to determine the strategic direction of the school SEND policy and improvement plan. They will report to the Governing body and will have a Governor member assigned to them to oversee the work that they do, who will visit the school throughout the year. The SENCo will be most effective if they are part of the school leadership team, but this is not always the case. With the status of being part of the leadership team, change can be implemented along with the capacity for the time needed to do the SENCo role for the best possible outcomes for the pupils. The CoP states that the SENCo should have the time and resources to carry out their role. This will differ in each and every school due to the size of the school, the number of pupils on role, and the number and type of SEND that pupils have.

PROFESSIONAL DISCUSSION

Speak with your SENCo in school and find out:

- are they part of the leadership team?
- how do they work with their headteacher to develop school policy and the SEND improvement plan?
- what work do they do with their school governor?
- how many SEND pupils are on the register?

The responsibilities of the SENCo

The SENCo will oversee the day-to-day operation of the school's SEND policy. Although it is the SENCo's responsibility to oversee this, it is not their role to implement every aspect themselves or to undertake every task relating to SEND. It is important that everyone in school takes the responsibility of supporting SEND pupils and implementing provision in and outside the classroom. Some of the activities that the SENCo will carry out are:

- supporting the identification of pupils with SEND;
- tracking and monitoring progress of pupils with SEND;
- co-ordinating the provision for pupils with SEND;
- liaising with parents and carer of pupils with SEND;
- liaising with outside agencies and professionals such as the Local Authority, family support workers and Educational Psychologists (EPs);
- ensuring that all records relating to a school's SEND pupils are accurate and kept up to date;
- leading on the development and implementation of the SEND development plan, which should link in with whole school priorities.

Some expectations for the SENCo role:

- That the SENCo is part of the leadership team.
- The SENCo regularly informs the leadership team and the Governors (including the lead governor for SEND) on current and changing policy and practice.
- The SENCo has a clear vision for SEND provision and outcomes within the school.
- The SEND report meets the legal requirements and is published on the school website.
- The SENCo has received training and is knowledgeable on policy and practice.
- The SENCo is involved (and potentially takes a lead on) making decisions relating to staff deployment and the use of resources for SEND pupils.
- The SENCo is challenged by the Governors/lead governor for SEND about the learning, progress and the use of resources for SEND pupils.
- To ensure that all staff know and understand their role in relation to supporting and implementing provision for SEND pupils.
- To ensure that staff CPD needs are met through identifying training needs of teachers and support staff such as Teaching Assistants (TAs) and Learning Support Assistants (LSAs).
- To ensure that High Quality Teaching is taking place for pupils with SEND (discussed later in Chapter 8).
- Liaise with curriculum co-ordinators to ensure that the SEND pupils have access to every area of the curriculum, and that adjustments are made and resources that are needed to support this are available.

School need to ensure that they provide a SENCo time for:

- planning and co-ordination (away from the classroom);
- maintaining records;
- teaching pupils with SEND;

- observing pupils in classes;
- co-ordinating, managing and training Teaching Assistants (TAs) and Learning Support Assistants (LSAs);
- liaising with settings either side of transition periods: nurseries, primary schools, secondary schools and colleges.

For some smaller primary schools, it may be appropriate that a SENCo is shared across schools, or that the role is part time.

CASE STUDY

From a primary school SENCo.

My days are never 'typical' as a SENCo, there is always something new or different happening, or something I need to find out, or a problem to solve. But, I have tried to outline some of the more typical elements of my day!

I have been a SENCo for many years, and my role has changed more recently. Years ago, I would have spent most of my time conducting reviews and writing targets, but now, as everyone is responsible for SEND, I take a much more creative approach to my role, which is both strategic and front line facing. I have a lot of mental health challenges to support and work with since the pandemic, and we are still working out the best way to support pupils with this as a school.

My day starts with arriving at the school and checking up on staffing and support changes and challenges, sickness cover, and emails that need attention first thing. As staff and pupils arrive at school, I greet pupils and parents and I check in with some of them to see how their morning has started. This can be a really important part to the day to gain an understanding of whether there may be any potential challenges that we have not accounted for. Once pupils are settled into their morning register, I return to the office to begin with paperwork and liaising with agencies regarding referrals that need chasing up or following up from, such as the Child and Adolescence Mental Health Team (CAMHS) or the Local Authority (LA) SEND team.

Today is Tuesday, and this is our day when I gather together the support staff (TAs and LSAs) during an extended assembly to deliver a short burst of training. It is something we have implemented recently to ensure that all staff are receiving the training that they need. Today I have designed some training on working specifically with small groups of pupils that have varying needs, and how to manage these groups better.

After break is my open-door policy, this is a time for staff to come and have a quick check in with me, often these sort of chats can fix a problem, just talking something through can generate a solution and they are really valuable. In between meeting with staff, I am working through paperwork and referral forms and beginning to draft the report for the upcoming governor meeting. My morning finishes with observing a pupil in class who is having difficulty with sensory needs and discussing some possible strategies for the teacher and TA to try out.

Over lunchtime, I check in with support staff that have been delivering morning interventions, and those preparing for delivering interventions in the afternoon. The afternoon

(Continued)

consists of supporting staff with review meetings. Some staff complete these on their own, others are finding these challenging, so we are doing them together as part of my work and training with class teachers. The end of the day finishes with a senior leader meeting, covering whole school aspects.

My job can be very challenging, frustrating and exhausting, but I also gain such a sense of fulfilment. Seeing the pupils develop and grow over their time with us and develop their confidence as learners inspires me to continue developing myself, and supporting others to develop and support pupils in their classes.

Reflect

- What do you think the SENCo role looks like for your SENCo in your current school?
- What do you think the main challenges are that they face?

The Roles and Responsibilities of the Class Teacher

The implementation of the new SEND Code of Practice in 2014, was very much about a shift in culture and practice. At the heart of the CoP lay the understanding of the need that every teacher should be responsible and accountable for every pupil in their class, including those with SEND. This was a monumental moment in the move from the SENCo taking the responsibility for all of these pupils, to everyone having a whole school responsibility. Some would argue that this was always the case in their schools, but for many it wasn't, so that by making this explicit, it has ensured that all pupils are gaining access to the support that they need from qualified specialists and teachers.

For example, it is the teacher's responsibility for all pupils in their class in regards to the progress that they make. If a pupil is taken out for an intervention, then the teacher should know what the intervention is, what skills or knowledge is being worked on, and how much progress is being made. It is not good enough for a teacher to say that they don't know, or to speak with an LSA or TA and ask them about a pupil. It is the teacher's responsibility to speak with the person delivering the intervention, and to assess a pupil themselves too. It is also really important that a TA or LSA does not work with SEND pupils all the time themselves. Every child has a right to have teaching and input from the class teacher, and TAs and LSAs also benefit from working with the wide range of attainment levels within a class. More will be discussed around these aspects in later chapters.

Being able to support your SEND pupils in the classroom will be an essential part of your job. As a trainee teacher, you need to begin to understand what your role will be, and how you will undertake this. It can be a challenge when you are juggling lots of elements of classroom practice such as planning lessons, marking work, and standing up in front of other professionals and being observed! But the sooner you begin to understand SEND and incorporate provision into your daily practice, the sooner this will become embedded. It is a key element of the Teachers' Standards, and learning about SEND and how to lead on this provision in your classroom is an entitlement within the Core Content Framework (CCF).

The number of SEND pupils that you have in your class will vary from school to school, and from year to year, but recent data (DfE, 2023) shows that for an average mainstream primary class, there will be approximately four to five pupils in each class that will need support for SEND; 2.5 per cent with an EHC plan and 13.5 per cent without, with an increase on the previous year (see Table 2.1).

One of the biggest worries for teachers is that they are not effectively supporting their SEND pupils, but research shows that the support that they gain from their classroom teacher has the greatest impact on the academic and social outcomes of their pupils with SEND (Efthymiou and Kington, 2017).

The Code of Practice (2015) outlines the responsibilities of the class teacher; these will seem vast at this stage of your journey, but be assured that you will be supported throughout your training year, and beyond this for a further two years as you continue to progress as an Early Career Teacher (ECT). These responsibilities are outlined below, and the link to the Code of Practice is in the further reading section of the chapter. You will not be expected to be an expert in all aspects of the teaching profession when you leave after your initial teacher training.

Table 2.1 The percentage of pupils with SEN support and EHC plans in primary schools (DfE, 2023).

Total SEN support		
	2021/2022	2022/2023
EHC plans	355,566	389,171
EHC plans (per cent)	4.0	4.3
SEN support/SEN without an EHC plan	1,129,843	1,183,384
SEN support/SEN without an EHC plan (per cent)	12.6	13.0
Headcount	9,000,031	9,073,832
State-funded primary		
	2021/2022	2022/2023
EHC plans	105,756	117,757
EHC plans (per cent)	2.3	2.5
SEN support/SEN without an EHC plan	606,086	629,184
SEN support/SEN without an EHC plan (per cent)	13.0	13.5
Headcount	4,655,513	4,647,851

Responsibilities of the class teacher

- Teachers are responsible and accountable for the progress and development of the pupils in their class, including where pupils access support from teaching assistants or specialist staff. *Include examples of this within your lesson planning.*
- The class teacher should remain responsible for working with the child on a daily basis, even when interventions involve group or one-to-one teaching away from the main class or subject teacher. *Include examples of how feedback from interventions inform your lesson planning.*
- The class teacher should work closely with any teaching assistants or specialist staff involved, to plan and assess the impact of support and interventions and how they can be linked to classroom teaching. *Include examples of this within your lesson planning.*
- Working with the SENCo, the class teacher should revise the support in light of the pupil's progress and development, deciding on any changes to the support and outcomes in consultation with the parent and pupil. *Include examples of this in your weekly mentor meetings.*

Class teacher responsibilities can be categorised under the three headings below.

- Directly to pupils at risk of or with special educational needs/disabilities (e.g. identification, assessment, intervention, monitoring and review).
- Working with families.
- Working with other professionals.

Activity

Open your copy of the Core Content Framework (CCF). As you read through the next section, highlight where it is explicit that you will be gaining training in these areas. Which areas will you be receiving direct training on, such as taught sessions from your training provider, or reading, such as working through this book and the related tasks? And which areas you will be working with your mentor or professionals in school on? – the 'learn how to' statements where you can discuss with practitioners and try out your practice with support.

In relation to pupils at risk of or with special educational needs/disabilities, class teachers should:

- ensure early identification of: special educational needs; barriers to learning; appropriate interventions and actions (e.g. the graduated approach which is discussed in Chapter 8) in consultation with the SENCo;
- have full knowledge of children's SEND support or Education, Health and Care Plans;

- provide access to a broad and balanced curriculum;
- understand and provide high-quality teaching;
- have appropriate high expectations based on assessment;
- assume responsibility and accountability for their learning, progress and development;
- maintain responsibility for working with them on a daily basis, even when interventions involve group or one-to-one teaching/support away from the main class;
- Regularly assess, monitor and review their progress (academic, developmental and social-emotional) during the course of the year with a view to ensuring the ultimate outcome of a successful transition to adult life;
- through professional development, secure knowledge, understanding and skills around: identification of specific special educational needs in the context of monitoring all pupils' progress and development; appropriate basic or advanced understanding of specific special educational needs/disabilities; quality teaching for pupils with special educational needs.

Class teachers should apply the graduated approach (as outlined in Chapter 8) to suspected special educational needs pupils in consultation with the SENCo (and Designated Teacher if the pupil is 'looked after' by the local authority), parents/carers and young people. As a trainee teacher, you will be shadowing your mentor at first, then working with them, then leading on elements such as these depending on which stage of your course and training and development you are at.

They should:

- Confirm delivery of high-quality teaching as a first step.
- Identify evidence-based interventions related to the pupil's special educational needs, implement them strategically and evidencing impact.
- Carry out a clear analysis of the pupil's needs based on all available evidence (e.g. school documentation of the pupil's progress to date with reference to national and peer-group data).
- Assess pupil needs formally and informally (including parents'/carers' and pupils' views).
- Where necessary, gain more specialised assessments from external agencies and professionals (as agreed with parents/carers).
- Decide about the level of special educational support required (with reference to the Local Offer and external agencies as necessary).
- Decide on the form and nature of any special educational support (with reference to the Local Offer and external agencies as necessary).

Class teachers should:

- Inform and involve parents/carers at the point of their and the SENCo's initial concerns about a child's learning and possible special educational needs.

- Develop a positive dialogue with them around their child's special educational needs, progress and outcomes.
- Be aware of how to handle any potential informal complaints.
- When a pupil is receiving SEND support, talk to parents regularly in addition to general best practice (i.e. meeting with them three times per year; and must produce an annual report on pupil progress).
- EHCPs should be reviewed at least once per year. There should be no time when parents are unaware of a school's concern that their child has special educational needs. The teacher and the SENCo (and Designated Teacher if the pupil is 'looked after' by the local authority) should agree in consultation with the parent and the pupil:
  - the adjustments, interventions and support to be put in place;
  - the intended impact on progress, development or behaviour;
  - involvement of specialists;
  - a clear date for review. Parents should be given clear information about the impact of the support and interventions provided, enabling them to be involved in planning next steps.

Working with families, class teachers must:

- Formally notify parents where it is decided to provide a pupil with SEND support, although parents and pupils should have already been involved in forming the initial assessment of needs.
- Contribute at least annually to an EHCP review where necessary.
- Produce an annual report on pupil progress.

Working with other professionals:

- The SENCo (and Designated Teacher if the pupil is 'looked after' by the local authority) should advise and support the class teacher in assessment, problem-solving and the effective implementation of support.
- Working with the SENCo (and Designated Teacher if appropriate), class teachers should revise a pupil's support in light of their progress and development, deciding on any changes to the support and outcomes in consultation with the parent and pupil.
- Teachers and support staff who work with the pupil should be made aware of their needs, the outcomes sought, the support to be provided and any teaching strategies or approaches that are required.
- Teachers should work closely with any teaching assistants or specialist staff involved, to plan and assess the impact of support and interventions and how they can be linked to whole-class teaching. Teachers should work with the SENCo to identify patterns in the identification of SEND.

- Teachers should work collaboratively with other professionals (including those from other disciplines) to improve special educational needs identification and support (e.g. approaches, strategies, resources, outcomes, review dates, etc).

Code of Practice (2015)

Chapter 7 will have a direct focus looking in detail at working with other professionals such as those outlined in the above section.

Activity

Review your highlighted CCF document. Can you generate some actions from this where you gain further experience to observe, shadow or lead on something that may be coming up? For example, a conversation with a parent or a review meeting.

Reflect

It is important to remember at this stage in your training that:

- Teachers have a responsibility to know about any additional support that a pupil may be having.
- Teachers need to understand the progress that their SEND pupils are making, and how this relates to their other lessons in class.
- Teachers need to understand that their SEND pupils should have fair and equal access to them as a class teacher during lessons.
- Teachers need to understand that although TAs and LSA make an excellent contribution to the progress of SEND pupils, it is their responsibility for the progress of their pupils. Support from other staff should supplement and not replace the class teacher.

Some of the other areas of the roles and responsibilities will be unpacked further and revisited as we progress through the chapters in the book.

Managing Classes with a High Number of SEND Pupils in them

As you have just read, for an average mainstream primary class, there will be approximately four pupils in each class that will need support for SEND. For some of you, this may seem a lot to manage; for others, you will have more than four pupils with SEND in your host placement class, and some classes may have up to a third or half of pupils with SEND that need additional support and resources. So, how do you manage this?

First, it is important to remember that you are a trainee teacher! You will become more expert as you move through your course and into your ECT years. Your mentor and your teacher training provider tutors will be there to guide you through each step of your journey.

There will be many challenges to working with a class with a high number of SEND pupils. You might be managing a larger number of support staff in your classroom; this will be looked at further in Chapter 7 when managing staff to support SEND pupils becomes a focus.

There will be further implications such as needing to consider the individual needs of pupils and potentially the additional time for planning and for the personalisation of needs, such as ensuring access to the curriculum, how pupils will be scaffolded to ensure that they can make progress. You will also need to think about how and when you will gain feedback and assessment from support staff to gather and put back into your planning, and when you will work with each of the pupils.

Key things to follow up on will be:

- How will you work with the additional number of adults in your class? This may include planning for TAs/LSAs and discussing plans and feedback from work they have been doing with pupils.
- Ensuring access to the curriculum for all pupils, through the use of scaffolding and adaptive teaching and planning for these adaptions.
- Ensuring that you work directly with all of your pupils to ensure that you have a good understanding of where your pupils are, and what progress they are making, and what gaps they may have. It is important that you take full responsibility for the progress of your pupils.

Challenges will be:

- Finding time to discuss plans, progress and assessment of pupils with your support staff. Build this into your day, are there times that you can check in with each member of support staff? Or during an assembly, or during your Planning, Preparation and Assessment (PPA) time?
- Adapting teaching for a larger number of pupils, considering individual needs and supports and scaffolds that will need to be in place. Seek support from experienced colleagues and your SENCo to ensure that you put appropriate scaffolds in place.

Each of these will be supported by your mentor, and you will not be expected to take on a class with a high number of SEND pupils on your own while you are in training. It will be good experience to work closely with your mentor, and you may have a focus group of SEND pupils that you work with initially and your mentor leads the other group. As you become more competent and confident, you will be able to take on further responsibility. As you move into your ECT years, you may work in a school that has particularly high numbers of SEND pupils in classes, and support for you as a developing ECT may be something that you would like to explore when visiting a school in preparation for a job application or at interview.

Chapter Summary

This chapter has outlined the long list of the roles and responsibilities of the SENCo as stated in the Code of Practice. It is important to understand the role of the SENCo, and how what you do within the classroom fits in to this larger model, and how the SENCo will be supporting you to support your SEND pupils. The chapter then progressed to outline your role as a teacher in relation to your SEND pupils, and again, there is quite a long list of elements for you to get to grips with as a trainee teacher – but you will be supported with this, and you will continue to progress and gain confidence as you move into your ECT years. This book will also support you with progression in your knowledge, understanding and developing your expertise as you move through the chapters.

The final section of the chapter considered the challenges of managing higher numbers of SEND pupils in class, and areas of this will be revisited and become a focus in the coming chapters.

Glossary of Key Terms

- NASENCO Award – National Award for SENCos; the qualification that SENCos must take within three years of undertaking the role as a SENCo.

Further Reading

- Department for Education (DfE) (2015). Special Educational Needs and Disabilities Code of Practice; 0 to 25 Years. DfE. https://assets.publishing.service.gov.uk/government/uploads/system/uploads/attachment_data/file/398815/SEND_Code_of_Practice_January_2015.pdf
- Department for Education (DfE) (2022). The Role of the Early Years Special Educational Needs Co-ordinator. DfE. https://assets.publishing.service.gov.uk/government/uploads/system/uploads/attachment_data/file/1059695/The_Role_of_the_Early_Years_SENCO.pdf
- Inside Government (2022). What is a School SENCo? Roles and Responsibilities. https://blog.insidegovernment.co.uk/schools/a-day-in-the-life-of-a-senco
- NASEN (2023). What is a SENCo? https://nasen.org.uk/page/what-senco

Links to the Teachers' Standards

- *2. Promote good progress and outcomes by pupils;* be accountable for pupils' attainment, progress and outcomes, be aware of pupils' capabilities and their prior knowledge, and plan teaching to build on these.
- *5. Adapt teaching to respond to the strengths and needs of all pupils;* have a secure understanding of how a range of factors can inhibit pupils' ability to learn, and how best to overcome these; have a clear understanding of the needs of all pupils, including those with special educational needs; those of high ability; those with English as an additional language; those with disabilities; and be able to use and evaluate distinctive teaching approaches to engage and support them.
- *6. Make accurate and productive use of assessment; know and understand how to assess the relevant subject and curriculum areas, including* statutory assessment requirements; use relevant data to monitor progress, set targets, and plan subsequent lessons.
- *8. Fulfil wider professional responsibilities;* develop effective professional relationships with colleagues, knowing how and when to draw on advice and specialist support; deploy support staff effectively; take responsibility for improving teaching through appropriate professional development, responding to advice and feedback from colleagues; communicate effectively with parents with regard to pupils' achievements and well-being.

Part Two: Personal and Professional Conduct

- 3. Teachers must have an understanding of, and always act within, the statutory frameworks which set out their professional duties and responsibilities.

References

Department for Education (DfE) (2015). Special Educational Needs and Disabilities Code of Practice; 0 to 25 Years. DfE. https://assets.publishing.service.gov.uk/government/uploads/system/uploads/attachment_data/file/398815/SEND_Code_of_Practice_January_2015.pdf

Department for Education (2023). Special Educational Needs in England Statistics. https://explore-education-statistics.service.gov.uk/data-tables/fast-track/c6a007df-e25d-444b-e4f8-08db6cc6d0f8

Efthymiou, E. and Kington, A. (2017). The development of inclusive learning relationships in mainstream settings: A multimodal perspective. *Cogent Education*, 4 (1).

Part II

Pupil Areas of Need

3

Communication and Interaction

Chapter Aims

- To gain an overview of the first broad area of need within the Code of Practice – Communication and Interaction.
- To gain detailed knowledge and understanding of Speech, Language and Communication Needs (SLCN) and associated literacy difficulties, linked to current research and theory.
- To develop an understanding of Autism Spectrum Condition (ASC).
- To develop an understanding of specific literacy difficulties.
- To gain an understanding of some supporting strategies for pupils with Communication and Interaction difficulties.

Links to the Core Content Framework (CCF)

Adaptive Teaching

- ***Learn that*** pupils are likely to learn at different rates and to require different levels and types of support from teachers to succeed.
- ***Learn that*** seeking to understand pupils' differences, including their different levels of prior knowledge and potential barriers to learning, is an essential part of teaching.
- ***Learn that*** adapting teaching in a responsive way, including by providing targeted support to pupils who are struggling, is likely to increase pupil success.
- ***Learn that*** pupils with special educational needs or disabilities are likely to require additional or adapted support; working closely with colleagues, families and pupils to understand barriers and identify effective strategies is essential.
- ***Learn how to*** receive clear, consistent and effective mentoring in supporting pupils with a range of additional needs, including how to use the SEND Code of Practice, which provides additional guidance on supporting pupils with SEND effectively.
- ***Learn how to*** identify pupils who need new content further broken down.

Managing Behaviour

- ***Learn that*** a predictable and secure environment benefits all pupils, but is particularly valuable for pupils with special educational needs.

Professional Behaviours

- ***Learn how to*** receive clear, consistent and effective mentoring in how to work closely with the SENCO and other professionals supporting pupils with additional needs, including how to make explicit links between interventions delivered outside of lessons with classroom teaching.

Introduction

What do we mean by 'Communication and Interaction' when it relates to the Code of Practice?

Some children and young people have Speech, Language and Communication Needs (SLCN), and this impacts on their ability to communicate with others effectively. It may be because they have difficulty with saying what they want to say or expressing their needs through communication. They may have difficulty understanding what is being said or asked of them. They may not understand the implied rules of social communication and interaction such as holding a conversation. Pupils may have all of these challenges, some of these challenges, or their challenges may change over time. Each of these aspects will be explored further in this chapter.

Needs around communication and interaction including the use of imagination and interpreting social situations can be a feature of specific areas of SEND such as specific literacy difficulties and Autism (also known as Autistic Spectrum Condition (ASC) and Autistic Spectrum Disorder (ASD); the term Asperger's or Asperger's syndrome is not used anymore and diagnosis for this is not given).

I will take this opportunity to note that in many cases with Autism, a diagnosis is given of Autistic Spectrum Disorder (ASD); however, the Autistic community prefer to be known as Autistic, or Autistic Spectrum Condition (ASC), as they do not like the connotations the word 'disorder' holds. You can read more about this in *The Neurodiversity Handbook for Trainee Teachers* (Alix, 2023). For this reason, I will be referring to Autism as 'Autism' or 'ASC' throughout this book, and not as a disorder.

When considering areas of need, and approaches to support a pupil, all areas of need should be considered, not just an area of primary diagnosis. The support should be based upon a full assessment of the pupil's strengths, areas of need, and appropriate well-evidenced interventions to target support for these areas of need.

We will now look at three key areas of Communication and Interaction in turn: Speech, Language and Communication Needs (SLCN); Autism; and Literacy Difficulties. SLCN may be linked to and be incorporated with the latter areas too.

Speech, Language and Communication Needs

Pupils with SLCN may have difficulty with various areas of communication. It could be a primary difficulty, or form part of another condition such as autism. Difficulties in this area can be misunderstood and mis-identified as behavioural difficulties and therefore it is important to gain a good understanding of this, the implications and strategies to support your pupils with SLCN in your own class. It could include difficulties with:

- forming sounds and words;
- fluency;
- formulating sentences;
- understanding what others say;
- using language socially.

Pupils experiencing difficulty in one of the areas above will have particular challenges in areas of the following:

- Attention and listening – pupils may have difficulty in listening to others, taking in what has been said to them, or concentrating on an activity or game for a short period of time. Pupils may jump from task to task without completing them.
- Play and interaction – SLCN may affect pupil play as they struggle to use language effectively to interact socially through their conversations and play. This could include difficulty in taking turns in a conversation, showing understanding towards the listener, or having a lack of eye contact.

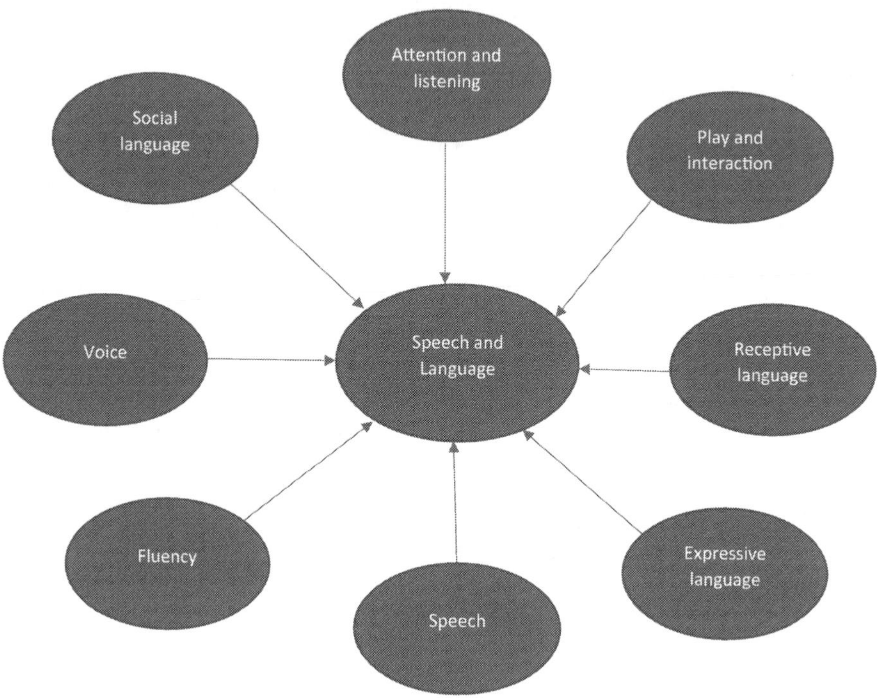

Figure 3.1 Diagram of the areas of challenge within speech and language development.

- Receptive language – pupils may have difficulty understanding the words that they are hearing, and what they mean. This can impact on them following instructions or completing tasks. There are many possible causes of a receptive language barrier, such as: developmental conditions, lack of exposure to language in the home environment, damage or trauma to the brain, a hearing or visual impairment, or a genetic or family link.
- Expressive language – pupils may find it difficult to express themselves and to be understood. This could be in relation to their ideas, their feelings or their needs and things that they want. They may have a reduced vocabulary against their age-related expectations, and have difficulty creating sentences or using the correct grammar.
- Speech – pupils may have difficulty with speech, meaning that they are hard to understand. They may have difficulty with discriminating between speech sounds. This could then impact on their play and social communication. There are four elements to speech production and pupils may have challenges with areas of these: correct breathing, phonation (causing the vocal chords to vibrate), resonance, and articulation (production of the sounds). This can also affect expressive language.
- Fluency – pupils may stammer or stutter in which whole words are repeated or segments or sounds, or there may be prolonged or repeated sounds, or they

may need to use additional effort to use speech. This often occurs between the ages of two and five years.
- Voice – a pupil may have an unusual voice quality such as hoarseness or harsh tones, and they may have frequent or persistent loss of their voice.
- Social language – pupils may have difficulty altering their use of language for their audience, for example speaking differently with a friend, to parents, and to a teacher.

Speech and Language UK have a good range of resources and Continual Professional Development (CPD); the link to their website is in the further reading section of this chapter.

Strategies to support pupils

- Ensure that pupils with SLCN are sitting near you so that you can easily and swiftly check in on their understanding.
- Ensure that you give pupils time for processing, this may be additional time to their peers, don't let them feel hurried to respond.
- Ensure that pupils feel confident and secure to be listened to, and that you will do your best to understand them. If you don't understand them, ask them can they say it in a different way, explain how we all learn differently and you may need a different way to understand.
- Model the correct way of saying something (rather than correct it).
- Make sure that your own use of language is simple, clear and direct. Keep sentences short and break down instructions into small chunks.
- Give a pupil with a stammer time to formulate their response, don't finish something for them.
- Focus on the content of what a pupil is saying rather than how the pupil is saying it.
- Use visual supports and manipulatives to support language and explanation.
- Improve your own use of non-verbal communication.
- Minimise environmental distractions such as noise.
- Teach new vocabulary explicitly through pre-teaching, or when vocabulary is being applied in a different context.
- If a pupil is having difficulty finding a word, offer the first letter or sound or ask them to describe what they are trying to say.

Many of these strategies should be 'ordinarily available' for pupils. This is applicable across each of the areas within this book. What is 'ordinarily available' is part of the Inclusive Teaching Framework. An example of this is given in the further reading section of this chapter.

Activity

Research what recommendations from your own Local Authority (LA) are given for 'ordinarily available' strategies and support.

Ordinarily available is the aim is to make high-quality teaching explicit, that it is available to all pupils, and that it is vital to some pupils, helpful to all pupils, and it is harmful to no pupils. Think about how these strategies align with these values.

Autism

What is autism, and how does it affect communication and interaction?

Autism is a processing difference. It is not an illness, and autism is not something that needs curing. It is a broad spectrum of different areas in which someone may have difficulties or challenges to varying degrees in each of these areas. The processing difference can have an impact on the person's life and the challenges that they face. Autistic people experience differences in areas such as: communication and language, social understanding, sensory processing, and flexibility in thinking.

The use of the word 'spectrum' can be very misunderstood in relation to Autism. People think of it as a length, and you are either on the lower end, or on the higher end. But this is not true at all. The spectrum is one of a profile of abilities, in which an individual may be more strongly affected in different categories – which is why one autistic person is very different to another autistic person. A really good explanation of this is given in the link at the end of the chapter (Autism; NeuroClastic). Lynch (2019) also looks at the spectrum of areas that can impact an autistic individual which goes beyond those outlined above.

Communication and language

There are differences in the way autistic people communicate and use language, and this can be seen in the interaction and development of their relationships. Some of your pupils may have no spoken language at all, and would likely be educated within a special school setting, and other pupils may be extremely talkative, particularly on topics that they are interested in.

The tone and volume of an autistic pupil's voice may also be affected, for example, they may have a monotone way of talking that lacks expression, or an overtly loud use of voice which appears inappropriate.

The interpretation of the language of others may also be problematic to autistic pupils. For example, many autistic pupils may have a literal interpretation of expressions that are used, such as 'pull your socks up' to ask a pupil to work harder and focus, or the use of humour, sarcasm or inference can be tricky for them and not understood. This then has implications for all aspects of communication, written and verbal. They may also appear direct in their own responses to questions or instructions that are asked of them, or they could come across as being rude in how they communicate with you.

You may have seen examples of this in class in which one of your pupils has misinterpreted something or taken something that you have said literally. You will need to consider what you might do differently for them, such as being clearer with your instructions or directions, rephrasing something, or giving an explanation on why that term is used, and what it means. You might need to check on your pupil's understanding of something you have said, as they may misinterpret it and not be doing as you have asked.

Social understanding

Autistic people experience challenges through not picking up on social cues or the unwritten rules and norms of social communication, such as turn taking during having a conversation or understanding if someone appears to be getting bored of a conversation topic. This can cause tension with peers, or when a pupil is working within a group.

Some pupils may prefer to work alone or with adults than their peers. This could be due to not wanting to be in conflict with peers, or because they prefer to be in control of their work, or because they feel more comfortable with the support of an adult or to be on their own.

Difficulties in social understanding can include the lack of eye contact during a conversation, or a pupil having an unusual or fixed eye contact. This could be that they are trying to conform to social norms, and they may feel uncomfortable giving or holding eye contact, but they realise that this is an expectation of 'normal' or a neurotypical social interaction. If a pupil is uncomfortable giving eye contact, they should not be forced or expected to, a pupil can listen and hear you without the need for eye contact. Some pupils may like wearing dark glasses inside to hide their eyes and shield them from eye contact.

Reflect

Consider a pupil who prefers to work alone than with their peers.

- What difficulties might you have with this in your class?
- Are there particular subjects in which you can make adaptations for, or are other subjects possibly going to be more difficult to enable to them to work alone during group tasks?
- What needs to be your focus when deciding whether to ask your pupil to work within a group?
- Is it the learning focus of the lesson, individual targets, or outcomes that you want the pupil to meet? It might be a combination.

Sensory processing

Everyone has sensory processing, but autistic people experience sensory difference which can impact on their behaviour. This can alter throughout the day and depending on their environment. Some pupils may have Sensory Processing Disorder (SPD) as a standalone educational need. Autistic pupils are highly likely to have some form of sensory processing challenges.

Sensory processing is a neurological process in which information is taken in through our senses and then organised so we can respond to it appropriately. This includes through smell, taste, touch, sound, vision, movement, body position, gravity. Neurotypical people use this information automatically and effectively. For people with SPD and autism, then, this can affect their daily lives including their behaviour, social interaction, education and work. Sensory processing is examined in more depth within Chapter 6.

There are two main types of sensory difficulties. First, hyper (over) sensitive and this includes fear of heights, avoidance of food textures, colours and temperature, avoidance of play equipment, fear of loud or sudden sounds, disliking touch such as hair brushing or washing, the shower and having nails cut. The second is hypo (under) sensitive. This includes appearing not to feel pain to temperature, seeking out movement such as rocking or fidgeting, chewing things and having poor awareness of the surrounding environment. However, they are interchangeable and pupils may be sensory seeking or sensory avoiding to gain stimulation or to remove themselves from it. This can change throughout the day, and affect concentration levels, and vary depending on the task and environment.

Reflect

Take a moment to pause. Imagine sitting in your classroom. Think about all of your senses in turn - what might you see, hear, smell, taste, touch, feel?

What does it feel like to be in your classroom when you take each of these in turn?

When you are next in your classroom, take moments in your day to pause and reflect on this.

What might your classroom be like for an autistic pupil with sensory processing disorder? We will look at some strategies to support them at the end of this section. When you read Chapter 6, take these thoughts and ideas, and extend them further.

Flexibility in thinking

Autistic people can be seen to have difficulties with flexibility in thinking. This can be associated in different ways. First, there is a difference in the interests of autistic people and your pupils and how they learn. They can become hyper-focused around special interests to them and put in a great deal of time and energy learning about a particular topic. They may be very uninterested in anything else that you might want to try and teach them.

Second, our pupils will be comfortable with routines and structure as this makes them feel safe, and they may like following classroom rules and structures. However, due to their inflexibility in thinking, this can cause them to become rule bound, fixating on rules and become upset by others that are seen to break them. It could be something like cheating in a game of football or when playing a board game, or by not putting a hand up to ask a question in class. At times, as a teacher, you may want some flexibility in some of these rules depending on the situation, but your autistic pupil may see this as being unfair and become distressed by it. You may need to consider your own school rules, or rules within the classroom. Think about when you might need to bend the rules for your pupils, and why. You may need to prepare an autistic pupil for this, or give clear explanation on why this might happen, or why it wouldn't happen in more serious situations such as breaking the law. It can be a complex area to explore, and you may need to think carefully about being flexible with rules in one situation, such as playing a friendly game in the playground, and being strict with rules in a tournament or sports game match.

Imaginative play can pose a difficulty for autistic pupils. However, this could vary in how you see it. Pupils may prefer role play that is very much based around situations that they know and understand, but they may not want to use objects or equipment that does not look or feel real. Some pupils may not want to join in with superhero games, but others will. It is important to remember that all autistic pupils are unique and very individual in their characteristics and how these impact on their behaviours and challenges.

Strategies to support pupils

- Use structure and routine within your teaching and your classroom.
- Know your pupils' individual differences.
- Consider your own use of language. Have you been specific, direct, and are instructions given in small chunks? Have you avoided humour, sarcasm, or overly long instructions?
- Use visual supports in teaching, this can be supported through the use of 'dual coding' (read more from Rosenshine and Sherrington (2019) who you will have come across already on your teacher training course). There is a link in the further reading section of this chapter to support the understanding and implementation of dual coding.
- Consider whether any sensory issues may need to be considered. Incorporate sensory breaks if needed.
- Do not hold the same social expectations and norms for autistic pupils as you do for other pupils. It is ok for a pupil to want to spend break time on their own taking a rest break from the social activity that has taken place within the classroom.

Literacy Difficulties

There is a clear relationship between SLCN and literacy difficulties. These difficulties can prove challenging when pupils are tackling phonics, reading and spelling. Further difficulties such as the understanding of language and what is being presented both in written form and verbal form can lead to challenges with reading comprehension. Pupils that are having difficulties with expressive language or spoken language may also have difficulties with developing written work. These areas could have an impact beyond when intervention to support SLCN has been in place and improvements have been seen.

Dyslexia

Primary schools may or may not screen for dyslexia. Dyslexia screening tools are often not used until a pupil is aged around seven to eight years old. Where screening tools are used, this is not a diagnosis; it is an indication of the areas of need for a pupil, and it will give a rating of whether dyslexia is probable or not. These tools then indicate what areas of support and intervention to focus on for a pupil, and this will be the same regardless of whether a pupil has a diagnosis or not. It is important to note at this point, that this is the same for any barrier or challenge that a pupil is having. Having a diagnosis or not does not affect the support that should be given to a pupil. If a child needs particular support in an area, then this should be implemented. Some literacy difficulties may relate to dyslexia, but some may not.

Throughout this section, I will be using a combination of 'person with dyslexia' and 'dyslexic'. Currently, there is debate whether this should be person first, like there was similar debate with someone being 'autistic' or 'someone with autism'. Always be mindful to refer to someone how they wish to be referred to, as the debates will continue for some years to come.

Here is a brief overview of dyslexia. Dyslexia can co-occur with other learning differences and can run in families. Dyslexia primarily affects the difficulty in reading and writing; however, there are many more areas of difference within someone that has a dyslexic brain. Dyslexic people (or people with dyslexia) may process information differently and they may find it challenging to remember information or have difficulty with their organisational skills. Dyslexic people can have strengths in areas such as the creative fields. For the purpose of this chapter, we are going to focus on the elements that affect literacy directly. The British Dyslexia Association (2010) has adopted the Rose (2009) definition of dyslexia.

> Dyslexia is a learning difficulty that primarily affects the skills involved in accurate and fluent word reading and spelling. Characteristic features of dyslexia are difficulties in phonological awareness, verbal memory and verbal processing speed. Dyslexia occurs across the range of intellectual abilities. It is best thought of as a continuum, not a distinctive category, and there are no clear cut off points. Co-occurring difficulties may be seen in aspects of language, motor co-ordination, mental calculation, concentration and personal organisation. Dyslexic readers can show a combination of abilities and

difficulties that affect the learning process. Some also have strengths in other areas, such as design, problem solving, creative skills, interactive skills and oral skills.

There are different types of dyslexia:

Phonological dyslexia – when there is difficulty remembering letter names and sounds which impacts upon blending and reading.

Surface or morphemic dyslexia – when there is an over reliance on phonology and the alphabet to read and spell. Irregular and sight words can be difficult due to this.

Hyperlexia – when there is a good memory for sight words and for blending; however, the understanding and comprehension of a text or what they have written may be poor.

Strategies to support pupils

- Multi-sensory teaching to support memory of letters and sounds.
- The use of structured Systematic Synthetic Phonics (SSP) programmes.
- Build in opportunities for revisiting learning frequently.
- The use of teaching spelling and handwriting, the conscious forming of letters alongside breathing, use of the lips and tongue to reinforce all aspects of letters and sounds will deepen and support learning.
- Consider how pupils are recording information, what is the focus of the lesson, can pupils use ICT methods instead?
- Present materials on coloured paper, this can make it easier to read words.
- Focus on content of feedback rather than picking up on every spelling mistake made as this can lower self-esteem.
- Do not ask pupils to read aloud in class, support reading 1:1 instead.
- Copying from the board can be difficult to navigate, looking up and back down, pupils can lose their place easily. Provide printed work.
- Pupils can struggle with generating or noting down ideas, the use of a scribe or buddy can be useful.

The Role of the Speech and Language Therapist

Speech and Language Therapists (SLTs) are health professionals who work with parents, carers, teachers, nurses, and doctors. As part of their role, they:

- support and care for children and adults who have communication difficulties, and/or difficulties with eating, drinking and swallowing;
- assess and work with people to improve difficulties with communication;
- develop personalised plans of support;
- work with children with difficulties such as a stammer.

In school, you may have someone supporting the SLT through providing recommended interventions for a pupil, or working on a different aspect of support such as social communication which an SLT does not work with as part of their role.

CASE STUDY

From Anna who is a SENCo within a small primary school.

Aamir is in Year 4. He has an EHC plan focused around his Speech, Language and Communication Needs (SLCN), he also has a diagnosis of Autism and has dyslexia indicators on a recent school screening assessment.

Aamir has a plan in place to support areas of his learning, some of which are through additional interventions. These include a social skills group in which pupils are facilitated in playing board games, which is supporting Aamir with social interaction such as turn taking and developing conversations around a game. It is also supporting Aamir with the use of rules, and how to react and control behavioural challenges when things don't go to plan and other pupils break the rules.

I am working with Aamir's current teacher who is a recently qualified teacher, an Early Career Teacher (ECT) on implementing supporting strategies that will be useful for Aamir and should be 'ordinarily available' in the classroom.

Aamir has particular difficulty with:

- Formulating sentences
- Understanding what others say

We have decided to implement the following strategies in the classroom, alongside the interventions he is attending, and then to review these in half a term:

- Adults to give Aamir time for processing instructions and questions, this may be additional time to their peers, don't let him feel hurried to respond.
- If an adult doesn't understand Aamir, ask him can he say it in a different way, explain how we all learn differently and you may need a different way to understand.
- Make sure that adults in the classroom use language that is simple, clear and direct, keeping sentences short and breaking down instructions into small chunks.
- Implement the use of visual supports for Aamir, such as a visual timetable and key information of activities that happen normally throughout the day.
- Increase the use of manipulatives to support Aamir's language and explanation.
- Improve adults' use of non-verbal communication in the classroom.
- Teach new vocabulary explicitly to Aamir through pre-teaching, or when vocabulary is being applied in a different context, adding this to the planning for the lesson.

The ECT is incorporating these strategies into her daily planning so that she can consciously implement and apply them, as sometimes she forgets to take these opportunities when juggling her own classroom for the first time. We are going to review these each half term so that we can assess Aamir's progress and the ECT's progress of implementing the strategies.

PROFESSIONAL DISCUSSION

Consider the case study of Aamir and the ECT. Discuss with your mentor what strategies would be best for you to begin to incorporate into your practice as part of what is 'ordinarily available' to your pupils.

- Are there any strategies that would be specifically useful that would be vital or crucial for some of your SEND pupils?
- How might you review your progress of implementing these?

Chapter Summary

This chapter has looked at the first broad area of need as defined in the Code of Practice (2015): Communication and Interaction. There have been three main focus areas to this chapter: Speech, Language and Communication Needs (SLCN); Autism; and Literacy difficulties including dyslexia. Each section has given an overview of the area, what it may look like and how it may present for a pupil in your class, and then each section gives some key supporting strategies for pupils including what should be ordinarily available to them. You are directed to some further follow-up reading, some of which may be incorporated within your teacher training course such as Rosenshine's Principles in Action (Sherrington, 2019). There is a summary of the role of the speech and language therapist to conclude; you can consider what an SLT is able to do, and what you will need to do beyond this to support your pupils with SLCN within your class.

Glossary of Key Terms

- Autism – This is a processing difference. It is a broad spectrum of different areas in which someone may have difficulties or challenges to varying degrees. The processing difference can have an impact on the person's life and the challenges they face. Autistic people experience differences in areas such as: communication and language, social understanding, sensory processing, and flexibility in thinking.
- Dyslexia – Dyslexia primarily affects the difficulty in reading and writing; however, there are many more areas of difference within someone that has a dyslexic brain. Dyslexic people may process information differently and they may find it challenging to remember information or have difficulty with their organisational skills.
- Ordinarily available – This is the aim to make high-quality teaching explicit, such that it is available to all pupils, vital to some pupils, helpful to all pupils, and harmful to no pupils.
- Sensory processing – This is a neurological process in which information is taken in through our senses and then organised so we can respond to it appropriately. This includes through smell, taste, touch, sound, vision, movement, body position, gravity.

- Speech and Language Therapists (SLTs) – Health professionals who work with parents, carers, teachers, nurses and doctors.
- Speech, Language and Communication Needs (SLCN) – The barriers to communicate with others effectively. It may include the difficulty with saying what is wanted to be said or expressing needs through communication.

Further Reading

- Alix, S. (2023). *The Neurodiversity Handbook for Trainee Teachers*. London: Sage.
- Autism Education Trust. https://www.autismeducationtrust.org.uk/
- British Dyslexia Association. https://www.bdadyslexia.org.uk/dyslexia/neurodiversity-and-co-occurring-differences/developmental-language-disorder-dld
- Council for Disabled Children, Speech, Language and Communication Needs Resources. https://councilfordisabledchildren.org.uk/what-we-do-0/networks/early-years-send/early-years-send-partnership-resources/speech-language-and
- Education Corner (2023). Dual Coding: The Complete Guide for Teachers. https://www.educationcorner.com/dual-coding-theory/
- Education Endowment Foundation (EEF). Special Educational Needs in Mainstream Schools, report and resources. https://educationendowmentfoundation.org.uk/education-evidence/guidance-reports/send
- Essex County Council. *Ordinarily Available Framework*. https://schools.essex.gov.uk/pupils/SEND/Pages/Ordinarily-Available.aspx
- Lynch, C. (2019). 'Autism is a Spectrum' Doesn't Mean What You Think. NeuroClastic. https://neuroclastic.com/its-a-spectrum-doesnt-mean-what-you-think/?fbclid=IwAR10zTutk4JTgRoLhTWdNEBRhbw4ch46Y5iKrDWjLFkGb7C1GMgV56f16fk
- Sensory Processing Disorder UK. https://thesensoryseeker.com/sensory-processing-disorder-in-the-uk/
- Speech and Language UK. https://speechandlanguage.org.uk/talking-point/for-professionals/the-communication-trust/

Links to the Teachers' Standards

- *2. Promote good progress and outcomes by pupils;* be aware of pupils' capabilities and their prior knowledge, and plan teaching to build on these; demonstrate knowledge and understanding of how pupils learn and how this impacts on teaching.
- *5. Adapt teaching to respond to the strengths and needs of all pupils*; have a secure understanding of how a range of factors can inhibit pupils' ability to learn, and how best

to overcome these; have a clear understanding of the needs of all pupils, including those with special educational needs; those of high ability; those with English as an additional language; those with disabilities; and be able to use and evaluate distinctive teaching approaches to engage and support them.

- *8. Fulfil wider professional responsibilities;* take responsibility for improving teaching through appropriate professional development, responding to advice and feedback from colleagues.

References

Alix, S. (2023). *The Neurodiversity Handbook for Trainee Teachers*. London: Sage.

Lynch, C. (2019). 'Autism is a Spectrum' Doesn't Mean What You Think. NeuroClastic: https://neuroclastic.com/its-a-spectrum-doesnt-mean-what-you-think/?fbclid=IwAR10zTutk4JTgRoLhTWdNEBRhbw4ch46Y5iKrDWjLFkGb7C1GMgV56f16fk

Rose, S.J. (2009). Identification and Teaching Children and Young People with Dyslexia and Literacy Difficulties: An Independent Report from Sir Jim Rose to the Secretary of State for Children, Schools and Families. London: Department for Children, Schools and Families.

Sherrington, T. (2019). *Rosenshine's Principles in Action*. Woodbridge UK: John Catt Publishers.

The British Dyslexia Association (2010). https://www.bdadyslexia.org.uk/dyslexia/about-dyslexia/what-is-dyslexia

4

Cognition and Learning

Chapter Aims

- To gain an overview of the second broad area of need within the Code of Practice – Cognition and learning.
- To gain detailed knowledge and explanation of cognition and learning needs, linked to current research and theory.
- To develop an understanding of Moderate Learning Difficulties (MLD).
- To develop an understanding of Severe Learning Difficulties (SLD).
- To develop an understanding of Profound and Multiple Learning Difficulties (PMLD).
- To develop an understanding of Specific Learning Difficulties (SpLD).
- To gain an understanding of some supporting strategies for pupils with cognition and learning difficulties.

Links to the Core Content Framework (CCF)

Adaptive Teaching

- ***Learn that*** pupils are likely to learn at different rates and to require different levels and types of support from teachers to succeed.
- ***Learn that*** seeking to understand pupils' differences, including their different levels of prior knowledge and potential barriers to learning, is an essential part of teaching.
- ***Learn that*** adapting teaching in a responsive way, including by providing targeted support to pupils who are struggling, is likely to increase pupil success.
- ***Learn that*** pupils with special educational needs or disabilities are likely to require additional or adapted support; working closely with colleagues, families and pupils to understand barriers and identify effective strategies is essential.
- ***Learn how to*** identify pupils who need new content further broken down.
- ***Learn how to*** apply high expectations to all groups, and ensure all pupils have access to a rich curriculum.

Professional Behaviours

- ***Learn how to*** receive clear, consistent and effective mentoring in how to work closely with the SENCO and other professionals supporting pupils with additional needs, including how to make explicit links between interventions delivered outside of lessons with classroom teaching.

Introduction

What do we mean by 'Cognition and Learning' when it relates to the Code of Practice?

Cognition and learning is one of the four broad areas of need within the Code of Practice (2015). This area relates to pupils who are further behind in their learning than their peers and learn at a slower pace. To understand what is meant by 'at a slower pace' you will also need to have a good understanding of the age-related expectations for the pupils who you are working with, within each of the subject areas you are teaching.

The Code of Practice (2015) states:

> *Pupils who demonstrate features of moderate, severe or profound learning difficulties or specific learning difficulties, such as dyslexia or dyspraxia, require specific programmes to aid progress in cognition and learning.*

We will be looking at these areas in detail over the course of this chapter.

Cognition is the process of something being learnt and is the acquisition, storage, retrieval and then the use of knowledge. Cognition is fundamental for learning to take place.

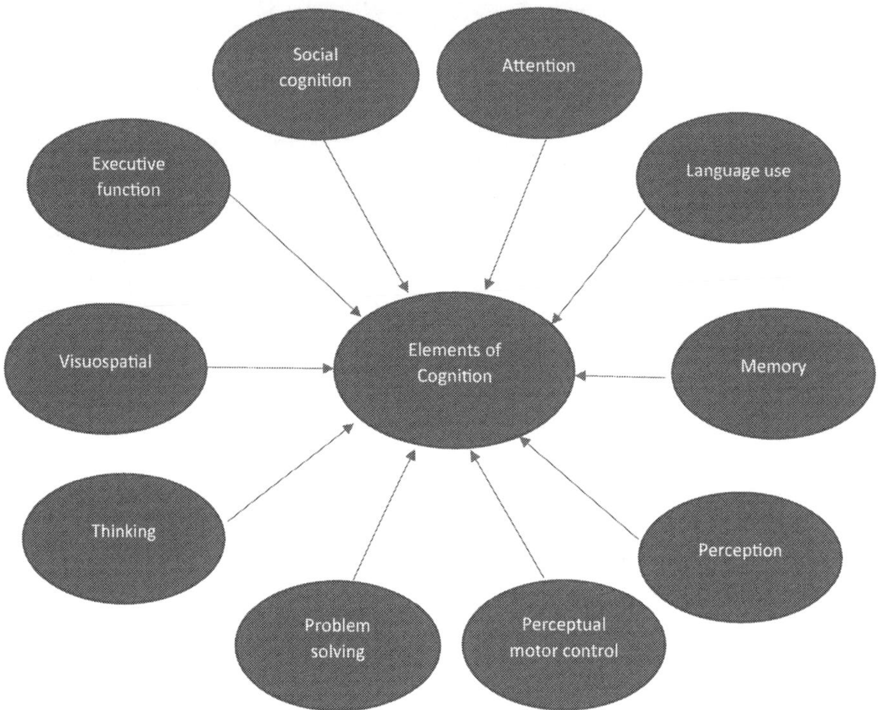

Figure 4.1 Diagram of the areas of elements of cognition.

There are many elements to cognition, and depending on what you read, models will include elements of the following:

- Attention – applying the mind to a focused consciousness that is of interest. This includes sustained, divided and selective attention.
- Language use – a shared language of learning, such as metacognition is useful here. Elements of language such as receptive language as seen in Chapter 3.
- Memory – including the sensory memory, short-term and long-term memory.
- Perception – understanding a broader context in which areas can be applied, predicting possible outcomes.
- Perceptual motor control – visual perception, reading and motor co-ordination.
- Problem solving – the identification of things that are not working, and then deciding upon a course of action.
- Thinking – forming models and associations of the world around us.
- Visuospatial – the ability to analyse and manipulate objects.
- Executive function – includes planning, decision making and flexibility.
- Social cognition – recognition of emotions, theory of mind, and insights.

As you can see, cognition is complex, and the impact of having challenges in one or more of these areas can significantly impact on learning.

We will now look at four key areas of Cognition and Learning in turn as outlined in the Code of Practice: Moderate Learning Difficulties (MLD); Severe Learning Difficulties (SLD); Profound and Multiple Learning Difficulties (PMLD); and Specific Learning Difficulties (SpLD).

Moderate Learning Difficulties (MLD)

Pupils with moderate learning difficulties have significant challenges in developing basic literacy and numeracy skills. They may also have other areas of development which are behind their peers, such as having a speech and language delay, a lack of social skills, poor concentration, and low self-esteem. Pupil attainment will be at least two to three years behind their peers despite a range of appropriate interventions and support being implemented, and they will have a general delay, rather than having specific learning delays as outlined in one of the upcoming sections. Pupils with MLD generally attend mainstream schools, but some may attend a special school.

Reflect

Do you currently have any pupils with MLD in your class?

- What are some of the challenges that they face as learners?
- What challenges do you face as their teacher?

Consider the strategies that are listed in this chapter.

- Are you and your mentor using some of these?
- Are there further strategies at this stage in your training that you think may be beneficial to your pupils that you will begin to incorporate into your practice?

During training, you will mainly spend time in a mainstream primary school, but you may have the opportunity to visit, or have part of your practice in a special school. This section will focus on MLD and SpLD when looking at supporting strategies as further strategies for pupils with SLD will be very individualised and specific to their needs, and the strategies within the sections on MLD and SpLD are the most likely areas of cognition and learning that you will encounter on your training and as you progress to your first years of teaching.

Pupils with MLD will have some or all of the following:

- Difficulty understanding basic concepts.
- Problems acquiring basic skills in reading, writing, and numeracy, resulting in a lack of confidence in using and developing the skills they do have.

- A lack of logic.
- Poor problem-solving skills.
- An inability to generalise learning and apply it to new situations.
- Limited communication skills, coupled with immature social and emotional understanding.
- Poor fine and gross motor skills.
- Difficulty with personal organisation.
- Poor auditory/visual memory.
- Poor long- and short-term memory; difficulty remembering what has been taught.
- Speech and language delay.
- Social and behavioural difficulties.
- Sensory impairment.

Strategies to support pupils with MLD

- As a teacher, follow plans and advice that have been given by educational professionals such as an educational psychologist or speech and language therapist.
- Know and understand your pupils. Develop positive relationships with them and build on this to understand what will work best for them.
- Provide a clear routine for your pupils, include visual timetables and timelines.
- Make sure the targets given to your pupils are achievable and appropriate for the attainment levels. Consider their developmental levels rather than their age.
- Break tasks down into little parts or chunks. Give praise when steps are achieved.
- Give the learner clear and basic instructions, and don't give them too many directives at once.
- Use sand timers when giving specific tasks, this can support a pupil to focus for a period of time if they have difficulty with attention.
- To ensure that your pupil understands what has been said to them, ask them to recap the provided instruction in their own words.
- Adapt the curriculum with support from your SENCo, ensure that a broad and balanced curriculum is still in place, including school trips and events.
- Use a variety of methods to transmit knowledge and learning to the child, including multi-sensory approaches, to ensure that all of the child's senses are engaged during the learning process.
- Support memory through simplifying tasks and using meaningful materials which aid recall.
- Use a memory board.
- Work closely with your learning support assistant or teaching assistant. You are responsible for pupils' learning, but they will also work closely with pupils. Ensure that you check in with pupils and assistants each lesson and ensure that you deliver lessons to your MLD pupils.
- To assist your pupil in structuring their work, give them a writing frame.

- Use simple, clear, and direct language.
- Use supporting materials such as visual aids, concrete examples, and manipulatives.
- Reduce cognitive load on pupils during lessons, there is a section on cognitive load later in this chapter.
- Use technology to support learning.
- Use interventions to support social development.
- Use think-pair-share, in which pupils have a thinking partner to share ideas and challenge each other. Pairs can then be joined together to make larger groups.

Severe Learning Difficulties (SLD)

Pupils with severe learning difficulties will have a similar learning profile to those with MLD. However, their attainment levels will be significantly lower across the subjects. Pupils may attend mainstream school or a special school, but it will be likely that they will need an adapted curriculum with support. Pupils with SLD may have a specific diagnosis of a medical condition such as Down Syndrome, or they may have co-occurring conditions or needs such as autism or Attention Deficit Hyperactivity Disorder (ADHD). Pupils with SLD may also have difficulties with mobility and co-ordination, communication, and self-care.

Strategies to support pupils with SLD

Strategies would include those as outlined in the section on MLD, and then, in addition to this, specific focused personalised strategies would be outlined and planned for pupils with SLD.

Profound and Multiple Learning Difficulties (PMLD)

Pupils with profound and multiple learning difficulties have complex needs. They have a range of needs which may include physical and sensory impairments alongside cognitive impairments. They are likely to have complex needs which include mobility, severe communication difficulties, and need significant support with their learning and personal care from an adult. Pupils with PMLD are most likely to attend a special school setting and may communicate through simple language or through the use of signs and symbols such as a Picture Exchange Communication System (PECS).

Strategies to support pupils with PMLD

Strategies would include those as outlined in the section on MLD, and then, in addition to this, specific focused personalised strategies would be outlined and planned for pupils with PMLD which may include the use of a PEC System for communication.

Although pupils with SLD and PMLD are mainly taught within special schools, some pupils may have split schooling with part of the week in special school and part in mainstream school. This can be supported through schools and parents as they wish for their child to be part of the local community and to spend time with peers within their community. Sometimes pupils may be within a mainstream school setting all the time due to parental wishes, or due to the lack of special school places in the area if parents request a place at one.

Reflect

Do you have any pupils with SLD or PMLD in your mainstream school?

- What does the educational provision look like for them?
- How is the curriculum adapted?
- Are there any spaces within school that have been adapted for them?

Specific Learning Difficulties (SpLD)

A specific learning difficulty is when there is an area of cognition that is affected, and a pupil finds it particularly challenging. Assessments will highlight this difficulty and support can be tailored around this. Most commonly, SpLDs in school will be either dyslexia, dyscalculia or dyspraxia. Pupils with a SpLD may excel in other areas and subjects, and their attainment may be high for some things. SpLD may stand alone or be co-occurring with conditions such as ADHD or autism. Pupils may also have difficulty with short-term memory and organisation.

We have previously looked at dyslexia in Chapter 3; the next section will look at the other areas defined above: dyscalculia and dyspraxia.

Dyscalculia

Dyscalculia is a SpLD where there is a difficulty with mathematical learning, in particular arithmetical skills, or numbers. It can affect grasping concepts and number facts, and will affect accuracy and fluency in calculation. There could be shared difficulties with dyscalculia and dyslexia through poor working memory, number recognition and reversals of symbols (letters and numbers). It is often co-occurring with ADHD, dyslexia and/or dyspraxia, which is likely due to sharing cognitive features and processing involved.

Indications of dyscalculia include:

- difficulty counting backwards;
- a pupil being slow to carry out calculations;
- a pupil with weak mental arithmetic skills;
- a pupil who struggles with estimation;
- a pupil who has difficulty understanding place value;
- a pupil who has high levels of anxiety in maths;
- a pupil who has difficulty learning and recalling basic number facts such as number bonds, e.g. 7 + 3 = 10;
- a pupil who still uses fingers to count instead of using more advanced strategies (like mental maths);
- a pupil who finds it difficult to understand maths phrases like *greater than* and *less than;*
- a pupil who has trouble keeping score in sports or games;
- a pupil who has difficulty working out the total cost of items and can run out of money;
- a pupil who avoids situations that require understanding numbers, like playing games that involve maths.

CASE STUDY

From a class teacher.

Talia was a Year 2 pupil in my class. She was an excellent writer, she enjoyed reading fiction, and she had age-related verbal skills. However, she was having difficulty with maths which was becoming more prominent, and she was not keeping up with her peers. Talia loved coming to school and learning, and she tried her best to work out the maths problems. I observed that Talia could count the numbers on a dice, and on coins when working with money, but as the numbers increased, she easily became confused, and struggled to work out calculations. Talia also found it difficult to retain sequential knowledge of numbers, and how numbers related to each other.

I arranged to meet with the SENCo and discussed it with them, and as part of the graduated approach (which is outlined in Chapter 8), the SENCo and I also spoke with Talia's parents to gather further information and their views on her progress and difficulties with maths.

As Talia's difficulties appeared to be isolated to maths, we started with some additional intervention and support through a school programme and through a supported on-line

(Continued)

programme which helped to assess Talia's areas of difficulty within maths and work on these areas.

I put some additional strategies in place within our maths lessons, and within other lessons when maths was incorporated. These included:

- Further use of manipulatives within our class teaching which supported Talia through a visual and interactive level.
- A clear focus on the targets that had been set for Talia, which had been set with the SENCo, and I had discussed with the TA.
- Adapting the curriculum to where Talia needed to fill in the gaps and secure her learning and mastery.

Talia began to make progress filling in some of the gaps she had gained. The SENCo continued to work with Talia knowing that this would be a continued difficulty, and area of need for her as she progressed through education. The SENCo ensured that there was a clear transition to her next teacher, with hand over discussions centring on the areas of difficulty for Talia, and the strategies that were in place.

Dyspraxia (Developmental Coordination Disorder, DCD)

Dyspraxia is a form of Developmental Coordination Disorder (DCD) and is a common disorder affecting fine and/or gross motor coordination in children and adults. Individuals may vary in how their difficulties present, and they may change over time depending on environmental demands and life experiences.

An individual's coordination difficulties may affect how a person functions with everyday life skills and in education and employment.

Children may demonstrate difficulties with a range of tasks including self-care, writing, and riding a bike. As they progress into adulthood many of these challenges will continue and may affect tasks such as driving a car and home maintenance.

Movement can be difficult for pupils with dyspraxia. These difficulties could include:

- extra physical and mental effort needed to carry out movements that pupils without dyspraxia manage easily;
- poor spatial awareness which can result in tripping over and gaining bumps and bruises more easily than others;
- difficulty carrying out practical tasks as pupils find it more challenging to learn the movements required for this;
- movements may lack fluency and a pupil with dyspraxia may appear awkward in their movement;
- difficulty in transferring over physical fine and gross motor skills that pupils have learnt in one context, to another.

There may be a range of co-occurring difficulties such as time management, planning and personal organisation. Many people with dyspraxia also experience difficulties with memory and processing. Dyspraxia can also affect articulation and speech, perception and thought. This might present through a pupil with dyspraxia struggling to keep up with conversations or taking a long pause before answering a question. They may lack a flow to their conversation, and this may be classed as verbal dyspraxia.

Dyspraxia is thought to be caused by a disruption in the way messages from the brain are transmitted to the body. This affects a person's ability to perform movements in a smooth, coordinated way. This is a neurological difference in the way the brain processes information.

Strategies to support pupils with SpLD

- Follow plans and advice that have been given by educational professionals such as an educational psychologist.
- Know and understand your pupils, develop positive relationships with them.
- Work closely with your learning support assistant or teaching assistant. You are responsible for pupils' learning, but they will also work closely with pupils. Ensure that you check in with pupils and assistants each lesson and ensure that you deliver lessons to your pupils.
- Reduce cognitive load on pupils during lessons, as outlined later in this chapter.
- Use supporting IT such as spellcheckers, accessibility font and text to speech software.
- Limit copying directly from the board.
- Make resources dyslexia friendly, limit the amount of text used and break it into chunks using bullet points.
- Check instructions have been written down correctly such as homework.
- Allow extra time for tasks to be completed.
- Consider whether responses can be given in a format other than written, such as a presentation or illustration.
- Consider the use of a scribe.
- Provide support for handwriting such as pencil grips.
- Do not ask pupils to read aloud unless they are happy to do so.

PROFESSIONAL **DISCUSSION**

Discuss with your mentor whether you have any pupils with dyscalculia or dyspraxia in your host class.

- What do you need to consider for them?
- What supporting strategies are already in place for them?

If you do not have any pupils with dyscalculia or dyspraxia:

- Has your mentor had pupils with these SpLD before?
- If so, what strategies were useful in supporting them?

The 'Five-a-Day' Principle

The Education Endowment Foundation undertake educational research. They have produced a guidance report – 'Special Educational Needs in Mainstream Schools' – which indicates that supporting high-quality teaching improves outcomes for pupils with SEND. They outline five specific approaches that they have named the 'Five-a-day', which they have found to have a positive impact with SEND pupils in the classroom. They advise that 'teachers should develop a repertoire of these strategies, which they can use daily and flexibly in response to individual needs, using them as the starting point for classroom teaching for all pupils, including those with SEND'.

1 Explicit instruction – Teacher-led approaches with a focus on clear explanations, modelling, and frequent checks for understanding. This is then followed by guided practice before independent practice.
2 Cognitive and metacognitive strategies – Managing cognitive load is crucial if new content is to be transferred into students' long-term memory. Provide opportunities for students to plan, monitor and evaluate their own learning.
3 Scaffolding – When students are working on a written task, provide a supportive tool or resource such as a writing frame or a partially completed example. Aim to provide less support of this nature throughout the course of the lesson, week, or term.
4 Flexible grouping – Allocate groups temporarily, based on current level of mastery. This could, for example, be a group that comes together to get some additional spelling instruction based on current need, before re-joining the main class.
5 Using technology – Technology can be used by a teacher to model worked examples; it can be used by a student to help them to learn, to practise and to record their learning. For instance, you might use a class visualiser to share students' work or to jointly rework an incorrect model.

Education Endowment Foundation (EEF) (2021)

Activity

Carry out an observation, either in your host class, or in another class.

Focus on the *Five-a-day* principle.

Draw up a grid and note when you see this happening in the lesson.

- What does this look like within this lesson?

Carry out this activity again in another subject.

- What can you see that is transferable, and what looks different in the way it has been implemented? For example, how has flexible grouping, or the use of technology changed for each lesson?

Cognitive Load Theory

Throughout this chapter cognitive load has been mentioned. You may have already had some training on cognitive load as part of your teacher training course, and it will be outlined here. The Centre for Education Statistics and Evaluation (2017) reports in detail the theory around cognitive load theory. Working memory can be overloaded and therefore information can be lost as there are limitations on the capacity of it. The report outlines the three types of cognitive load:

- Intrinsic load – if the complexity of the material presented is too high, and the knowledge of the learner does not support this, then the cognitive load can be too much for the learner and not understood and retained. This will have a negative effect on learning.
- Extraneous load – when a learner is required to solve a problem on their own without skills or instruction to do this, the learner is focused on trying to solve the problem rather than the technique of how to do it (which they don't already have). This will have a negative effect on learning.
- Germane load – instruction is designed to support schema construction and learner progress. The instruction gives examples of how to work the problem out so this can be replicated when presented again. This will have a positive effect on learning.

As you can imagine, intrinsic and extraneous load on your SEND and neurodivergent learners can prove overwhelming and potentially cause challenges with exhibited negative behaviours, not coping, and low self-esteem. This is why it is important to know your learners and the complexity of the material to be included, and to have a robust understanding of pupils prior learning so that instruction can be tailored towards maximising the germane load (Alix, 2023).

Metacognition and Self-Regulated Learning

Metacognition has also been listed as an area to consider as a supporting strategy for learners. It is the process in which pupils think about their own learning and the choices that they make when they are learning. When support for metacognition in the classroom is implemented correctly, research has demonstrated it can make as much impact as an additional seven-month progress (EEF, 2018). Metacognitive strategies should be taught in conjunction with subject-specific areas to ensure the transference of skills.

Muijs and Bokhove (2020) examined studies on metacognition and self-regulated learning, and from these, they define metacognition as monitoring and control and knowledge, in which learners monitor and direct their own learning by using a strategy, monitoring whether it works, and adapting it or using it again depending upon the outcome. For example, looking at feedback and redrafting work, checking success criteria, deciding what went well, and whether you have to overcome any difficulty.

Self-regulation also includes monitoring and control and knowledge with cognition and motivation. They conclude that self-regulation focuses on the extent to which learners understand their strengths and areas for development, and how they use and develop strategies to support themselves to enhance their learning and progress. This can be developed with SEND learners to support their progress and taking ownership of their learning.

Further Support

It is important to note, that your pupils should not be defined by labels, and each of your pupils is unique. What strategy works for one pupil won't work for another, even if they have the same diagnosis or fall into the same category within the Code of Practice. What is more important is that you take the time to get to know each child as an individual, and find out what works for them, and what do you need to do, as their teacher, to support them to make the next steps of progress. A key way to do this is to take a step back and observe your pupil, either working on their own, or working with someone else or an adult. Consider: how do they approach a task when it is given? What behaviours do they show? What actions do they take? Can you see any patterns in how they approach tasks and instructions?

As you will already start to see, your pupils may not fit neatly into one broad area of need either. There may be cross overs between areas, or your pupil may have elements that fall in to two or more areas. So, what happens then? For the purpose of recording your pupil onto a special needs register, or when an applying for an Education, Health and Care Plan (EHC plan) (discussed in Chapter 9), then a pupil will be listed as being within one area of need. This is classed as their main area of need. But they may have other areas of need too, and these areas will still go on to their one plan, or EHC plan with targets relating to these areas. Again, it is not about labelling a pupil, it is about looking at what they need, what areas of support do they need, and then implementing a plan to support and address these areas.

Chapter Summary

This chapter has looked at the second broad area of need as defined in the Code of Practice (2015): Cognition and Learning. There have been four focus areas to this chapter: Moderate Learning Difficulties (MLD); Severe Learning Difficulties (SLD); Profound and Multiple Learning Difficulties (PMLD); and Specific Learning Difficulties (SpLD). Each section has given an overview of the area, what it may look like and how it may present for a pupil in your class, and then each section gives some key supporting strategies for pupils including what should be ordinarily available to them. The next sections of the chapter focused on the Education Endowment Foundation's Five-a-day principle, and for you to consider how this looks in practice within your class, and there is an overview of cognitive load and metacognition which are suggested areas to consider when implementing strategies for your SEND pupils.

Glossary of Key Terms

- Moderate Learning Difficulties (MLD) – Pupils will have attainment levels well below age-related expectations (two to three years) even with interventions and support being in place.
- Profound and Multiple Learning Difficulties (PMLD) – Pupils have severe and complex learning needs, combined with other significant difficulties such as physical or sensory impairments.
- Severe Learning Difficulties (SLD) – Pupils will have a significant cognitive impairment and will need support in all areas of the curriculum.
- Specific Learning Difficulties (SpLD) – Pupils will have a specific difficulty such as dyslexia, dyscalculia, or dyspraxia, but will have strengths in some areas of the curriculum.

Further Reading

- British Dyslexia Association. https://www.bdadyslexia.org.uk
- Dyspraxia Foundation. https://dyspraxiafoundation.org.uk/
- Education Endowment Foundation (EEF) (2021). Special Educational Needs in Mainstream Schools; Guidance Report. https://d2tic4wvo1iusb.cloudfront.net/production/eef-guidance-reports/send/EEF_Special_Educational_Needs_in_Mainstream_Schools_Guidance_Report.pdf?v=1690614961

- Education Endowment Foundation (EEF) (2021). High Quality Teaching Benefits Pupils with SEND; The five-a-day principle. https://d2tic4wvo1iusb.cloudfront.net/production/eef-guidance-reports/send/Five-a-day-poster_1.1.pdf?v=1690638622
- Education Endowment Foundation (2018). Metacognition and Self-Regulated Learning. https://educationendowmentfoundation.org.uk/education-evidence/guidance-reports/metacognition
- Education Endowment Foundation (2021). Cognitive Science Approaches in the Classroom; A Review of the Evidence. https://educationendowmentfoundation.org.uk/education-evidence/evidence-reviews/cognitive-science-approaches-in-the-classroom?utm_source=/education-evidence/evidence-reviews/cognitive-science-approaches-in-the-classroom&utm_medium=search&utm_campaign=site_search&search_term=cognitive%20science%20approaches%20in%20the%20classroom
- McGill, R. (2022). *The Teacher Toolkit Guide to Memory*. London: Bloomsbury.
- National Association for Special Educational Needs (NASEN) (2022). Teacher Handbook: SEND; Embedding Inclusive Practice. Education Endowment Foundation (EEF). https://www.wholeschoolsend.org.uk/resources/teacher-handbook-send
- The Centre for Education Statistics and Evaluation (2017). *Cognitive Load Theory: Research that Teachers Really Need to Understand*. NSW Department of Education.

Links to the Teachers' Standards

- *2. Promote good progress and outcomes by pupils*; be aware of pupils' capabilities and their prior knowledge, and plan teaching to build on these; demonstrate knowledge and understanding of how pupils learn and how this impacts on teaching.
- *5. Adapt teaching to respond to the strengths and needs of all pupils*; have a secure understanding of how a range of factors can inhibit pupils' ability to learn, and how best to overcome these; have a clear understanding of the needs of all pupils, including those with special educational needs; those of high ability; those with English as an additional language; those with disabilities; and be able to use and evaluate distinctive teaching approaches to engage and support them.
- *8. Fulfil wider professional responsibilities*; take responsibility for improving teaching through appropriate professional development, responding to advice and feedback from colleagues.

References

Alix, S. (2023). *The Neurodiversity Handbook for Trainee Teachers*. London: Sage.

Department of Education and Department of Health (2015). Special Educational Needs and Disability Code of Practice: 0 to 25 years. Statutory guidance for organisations which work with and support children and young people who have special educational needs or disabilities. Government Publications.

Education Endowment Foundation (2018). Metacognition and Self-Regulated Learning. https://educationendowmentfoundation.org.uk/education-evidence/guidance-reports/metacognition

Education Endowment Foundation (EEF) (2021). High Quality Teaching Benefits Pupils with SEND; The five-a-day principle. https://d2tic4wvo1iusb.cloudfront.net/production/eef-guidance-reports/send/Five-a-day-poster_1.1.pdf?v=1690638622

Muijs, D. and Bokhove, C. (2020). *Metacognition and Self-Regulation: Evidence Review*. London: Education Endowment Foundation.

The Centre for Education Statistics and Evaluation (2017). *Cognitive Load Theory: Research that Teachers Really Need to Understand*. NSW Department of Education.

5

Social, Emotional and Mental Health (SEMH)

Chapter Aims

- To gain an overview of the third broad area of need within the Code of Practice – Social, Emotional and Mental Health (SEMH).
- To gain detailed knowledge and explanation of Mental Health Difficulties, Attention Deficit Hyperactivity Disorder (ADHD), Attachment Disorder, Co-occurrence of needs, and Communication and behaviour, linked to current research and theory.
- To develop an understanding of mental health difficulties.
- To develop an understanding of Attention Deficit Hyperactivity Disorder (ADHD).
- To develop an understanding of attachment disorder.
- To develop an understanding of communication and behaviour.
- To gain an understanding of some supporting strategies for pupils with Social, Emotional and Mental Health (SEMH).

Links to the Core Content Framework (CCF)

High Expectations

- ***Learn that*** teachers are key role models, who can influence the attitudes, values and behaviours of their pupils.
- ***Learn that*** setting clear expectations can help communicate shared values that improve classroom and school culture.
- ***Learn that*** a culture of mutual trust and respect supports effective relationships.
- ***Learn how to*** acknowledge and praise pupil effort and emphasise progress being made.

Adaptive Teaching

- ***Learn that*** seeking to understand pupils' differences, including their different levels of prior knowledge and potential barriers to learning, is an essential part of teaching.
- ***Learn how to*** observe how expert colleagues adapt lessons, whilst maintaining high expectations for all, so that all pupils have the opportunity to meet expectations and deconstructing this approach.

Managing Behaviour

- ***Learn that*** the ability to self-regulate one's emotions affects pupils' ability to learn, success in school and future lives.
- ***Learn that*** teachers can influence pupils' resilience and beliefs about their ability to succeed, by ensuring all pupils have the opportunity to experience meaningful success.
- ***Learn that*** pupils' investment in learning is also driven by their prior experiences and perceptions of success and failure.
- ***Learn how to*** establish a supportive and inclusive environment with a predictable system of reward and sanction in the classroom.
- ***Learn how to*** work alongside colleagues as part of a wider system of behaviour management (e.g. recognising responsibilities and understanding the right to assistance and training from senior colleagues).

Introduction

What do we mean by 'Social, Emotional and Mental Health (SEMH)' when it relates to the Code of Practice?

Social, Emotional and Mental Health (SEMH) is one of the four broad areas of need within the Code of Practice (2015). This area relates to pupils who may be experiencing some form of SEMH. SEMH is wide ranging and may include mental health such as depression, anxiety, eating disorders, substance misuse and self-harm. SEMH may impact upon pupils and show through behaviours such as challenging, withdrawn, or disruptive behaviour.

Pupils may have a disorder or condition which impacts upon SEMH, or a co-occurrence with SEMH such as Attention Deficit Hyperactivity Disorder (ADHD), Autism, Obsessive Compulsive Disorder (OCD), Post Traumatic Stress Disorder (PTSD) or attachment. Diagnosis, awareness and understanding of SEMH needs is on the increase, and post-Covid there has been an increase of the impact of Covid lockdowns and restrictions on pupils' mental health.

The Department for Education (DfE) (2023) have introduced a training module on mental well-being. This demonstrates their understanding of the need to continue to develop this support for both pupils and teachers in school. Within the new mandatory health education curriculum, pupils are taught:

- How to recognise the early signs of mental wellbeing concerns, including common types of mental ill health.
- Where and how to seek support.
- Whom they should speak to in school if they're worried about their own or someone else's mental wellbeing.

DfE (2023)

Mental Health Difficulties

So, how will SEMH present?

There may be milder SEMH needs to more serious mental health conditions, which will all have a combination of different indicators. Things all school staff need to look out for or be vigilant of are outlined in Figure 5.1:

Pupils with SEMH needs are at risk of underachieving, missing school or being excluded and careful consideration of their mental health is vital.

PROFESSIONAL **DISCUSSION**

As part of your mentor meeting, discuss with your mentor and identify any pupils with SEMH needs.

Find out what support or interventions are in place for them, and how they are individualised for each pupil.

What other provision is available within your school setting?

I discuss the following areas in my book, *The Neurodiversity Handbook for Trainee Teachers* (Alix, 2023), in which I link the areas of need with a neurodiversity model.

Extracts from this are presented below to outline key areas of SEMH.

Figure 5.1 Diagram of the indicators of SEMH needs.

Anxiety

There are two main types of anxiety; generalised anxiety and phobias, which can be categorised further.

- Specific phobia – this is a fear of a specific thing, such as dogs, the dark or spiders. Pupils might avoid situations where they may come into contact with their phobia.
- Social phobia – this is an extreme phobia or fear of becoming embarrassed within a social situation. Pupils may be frightened to speak in front of other pupils or read aloud, and they may avoid school to prevent themselves from being placed in this situation.
- School phobia – this could be linked to social phobia, and it is the fear of going to school. It may be in relation to bullying incidents so this should be explored. It may also be related to unmet SEND needs or differences.
- Agoraphobia – is an extreme phobia in which the pupil has a fear of leaving the house and being in a public place.

- Separation anxiety – this is when a pupil is fearful of being left and may become distressed when being dropped off at school. This is often seen in younger pupils.
- Selective mutism – this is a result of extreme social anxiety; the pupil may feel as though they lose the ability to speak and cannot speak in a stressful situation. They have no choice or control of this, even though it is called 'selective'.

(Alix, 2023)

Some pupils may experience a 'panic attack' or 'anxiety attack'. Often, these terms are used interchangeably. However, they are distinct in the root of the trigger and when and how they present themselves. An anxiety attack is when the fear is related to the current situation, an anxiety of what is happening or about to happen. A panic attack is when someone experiences an attack at any time which may be unrelated to a current situation, and it may be difficult to identify the trigger (Alix, 2023).

Both may present with the same physical experiences and could include:

- a dry mouth;
- feeling in the stomach such as a churning or butterflies;
- the need to go to the toilet;
- a racing heart or palpitations;
- breathlessness or hyperventilating;
- nausea.

Anxiety can affect a pupil's behaviour and may show as: a pupil walking or running out of class to avoid the situation; the refusal to follow instructions as this may put them in a situation to cause them anxiety, or to be defiant to avoid the situation.

There are many possible triggers to pupil anxiety in school and these could include:

- the weather outside, storms and loud noises;
- insects in the classroom, as they have no control of moving away from them;
- large open spaces;
- crowded places and communal areas;
- being asked to read out loud in front of a class;
- speaking to the whole class;
- using school toilets: germs, space, other pupils being in there too;
- being ill, the fear of being sick;
- school vaccination programmes;
- tests and exams.

You also need to consider some of the above elements if you are taking pupils on a school trip outside of school, such as open spaces, crowds, weather, and insects. In addition to these, be aware of:

- travelling on public transport;
- the use of lifts and escalators.

Let's consider some further strategies to support a pupil with anxiety. First, prepare pupils for each lesson so that they know what to expect, the use of visual timetables or instructions can be useful here. Most primary schools use visual timetables for all pupils, but your SEMH pupils may need something more personal to them. This could be elements broken down further, or for someone to talk through this at the start of each day or at intervals throughout the day to give opportunities for discussion, questions, and clarification. Maintain routines so that pupils know what to expect each day. Sometimes changes in routine cannot be avoided in a school but try to prepare your SEMH pupils for any changes that you anticipate, and acknowledge that if there are changes to routines that this may cause some difficulty and consider how you might support your pupils through this. Use social stories to prepare the pupil for new situations that might be approaching, such as a school trip or transition to a new year group and explain the rules carefully and thoroughly so that pupils understand the expectations that lay within the rules.

CASE STUDY

From a pastoral lead.

Mateo had just started Year 3, and was attending a junior school. He had visited the school which was on the same site as the infant school on several occasions prior to starting Year 3, but he was finding leaving his grandmother, Amelie, very difficult in the mornings. Mateo showed signs of anxiety and stress as the school day approached in the morning which sometimes lead to tears and challenging behaviour. Amelie herself was becoming anxious and stressed by the drop off, and said it felt like going back several years to reception when Mateo was very difficult to settle into school and detach from his grandmother in the morning. I arranged a meeting with the SENCo, class teacher, previous class teacher and grandmother to discuss Mateo's situation, his needs, and some potential strategies to support him.

Mateo had some attachment issues as he had left his maternal mother's care at the age of three and gone to live with his maternal grandmother, Amelie, due to substance mis-use and neglect within the family home. Mateo had spent time being unsettled, and contact with his mum had been sporadic. His infant school worked with his grandmother when he transitioned into each year group to implement some strategies to support Mateo to leave her and settle in to the school day more easily.

At the meeting, these strategies were discussed. They included:

- a slightly earlier drop off before the school site became busy so that Mateo and his grandmother could come into the classroom earlier and work on some activities together, so that Mateo could settle in to the school morning;
- a selection of activities of Mateo's choosing that he could do with his grandmother;
- for the Teaching Assistant (TA) to be available to join in with activities and transition taking over from Amelie, so that she could leave;

(Continued)

- a phone call home to Amelie at break and lunch if needed so that Mateo could tell his grandmother what he had been doing at school, and seek reassurance that she would be returning to collect him at the end of the day.

As time progressed through each of the years at infant school, these scaffolds to support the transition could be taken away as Mateo became happy and confident in his relationships with the new class teacher and TA, and in his reassurance that his grandmother would return for him. It was decided that these strategies would be put into place for Mateo again, with the acknowledgement that this was a bigger transition as it was a change of school for him as well as year group. The school also needed to consider the funding to support the TA starting a little earlier each day, and they sought some transition funding for this.

I discussed the strategies with Mateo so that he could see there were check-in points throughout the day with his grandmother. In the second part of the autumn term, the majority of the scaffolds had been removed, phone calls were no longer needed, and Mateo arrived only fifteen minutes early so that he had time to settle before the classroom became busier. This strategy stayed in place all year.

Reflect

Reflect on the case study of Mateo and his grandmother.

- How may the transition from the infant school to the junior school have been made easier for Mateo?
- What might you have wanted to put into place prior to him moving school?
- If you were Mateo's teacher now, what transition support would you be considering for his next transition into Year 4?

Depression

Being sad or a little bit down is a normal emotion that we all feel. These feelings vary at different times throughout our lives, and they can even fluctuate across a day, a week or month. We need to become concerned if the low feeling or mood becomes more persistent or starts to become overwhelming.

Depression responds well to medical treatments, and therefore it is important to direct pupils and parents or carers for medical support and assessment.

There can be many causes to depression or a depressive episode:

- Extreme adverse circumstances in the pupil's life which may be: trauma, abuse, bereavement, loss, illness.
- Being lonely or isolated.

- Developing identity such as gender, sexuality, cultural or religious.
- Hormonal changes.

Depression can co-exist with other SEND areas of need such as autism and ADHD.

There are warning signs of depression that you may see in a pupil in your class:

- Unusual sad or low moods that don't disappear.
- Being overly self-critical.
- Not having any energy, which may lead to a loss of interest in normal activities.
- Irritable or angry.
- Neglecting personal hygiene.
- Changes in sleep or appetite.
- Participating in risky behaviours.
- Self-harm.

OCD

Obsessive Compulsive Disorder (OCD) can include obsessive thoughts, fears and anxieties, and the compulsion to carry out certain behaviours to make the person feel safe. For example, cleaning hands or surfaces, repeating something in a ritualistic way such as locking and relocking a door or checking something has been switched off. Younger pupils who have OCD tend to find that the behaviours become milder or disappear as they get older.

OCD can be very debilitating with the difficulty for the pupil to attend school, complete homework or leave the house, resulting in high levels of absence. A pupil may also be worried and embarrassed by their compulsive behaviours. Other forms of OCD may include: hair pulling, skin picking, tics and Tourette's and body dysmorphia. Again, these can co-exist with other SEND areas of need.

PTSD

Post-Traumatic Stress Disorder (PTSD) occurs due to an event that has caused a long period of fear or anxiety for a child. A pupil may withdraw from others (peers and adults). They may have a sense of hyperarousal in which a pupil is on high alert and in a fight or flight mode the majority of the time. For younger pupils, the brain could be altered as it is developing to act in response to constant fear.

A pupil may show the effects of PTSD by:

- finding it difficult to explain or understand feelings;
- having difficulty making and maintaining relationships;
- having the inability to trust adults;
- having poor concentration;
- having angry outbursts;

- having a lack of the sense of safety;
- having a lack of social skills;
- being fearful of failure.

A pupil will need:

- additional support and care;
- self-esteem development.

PTSD can have an impact on pupil behaviour. If a pupil is angry (which could be demonstrated across the range of SEMH needs), this could be due to the changes of the chemicals in the brain, or changes within the pathway structures of the brain. They are reacting to something that may have happened, and this is their survival mode. You may need to additionally support a pupil through giving them time and space to listen to them, use active listening to show them that they matter and that their problems and concerns are important to you and you want to support them. Talk about feelings, this could be part of a whole class strategy that you use, or part of PSHE lessons. You may need to refer them to more specialist support in school from a learning mentor or a pastoral support team. This will vary from school to school depending on what resources are in place, and how pastoral teams are structured. Find out from your host school what this looks like. Give opportunities for a pupil to release frustration, for example through sport during break times and after school in addition to PE lessons. Introduce meditation techniques or mindfulness, again as part of whole class strategies, or individual support and time when needed.

Attention Deficit Hyperactivity Disorder (ADHD) and Attention Deficit Disorder (ADD)

Although ADHD is categorised within SEMH needs, it could be argued that this could be situated within other areas such as cognition and learning.

The diagnostic label is ADHD, but the ADHD foundation suggest that, as with autism, ADHD should now be reframed, and behaviours are often referred to as 'dysregulation' for this and other associated behaviours. The term condition is also suggested as an alternative for disorder, but this is yet to become more widespread, as is the case with autism.

ADHD can impact on a learner's development, and they can have a delay of two or three years in comparison to their age-related expectations. One of the main characteristics of ADHD is challenges that pupils will have relating to their emotional self-regulation, which is why the term dysregulation is applied.

Associated behaviours of ADHD are:

- dysregulation of behaviour;
- attention;

- easily distracted;
- coping problems;
- depression;
- co-occurrence with other conditions such as autism and SpLD.

Boys tend to be diagnosed with ADHD, and with further research in girls (as with autism) more is becoming known about ADD in girls, who tend to lack the hyperactivity element, but can result in a lack of coping mechanisms in life.

ADD can also be referred to as ADHD – I (ADHD – inattentive). It refers to when a pupil (normally a girl) has difficulty in paying attention, staying organised, and managing their time and prioritising. But, they do not show the element of hyperactivity. They do not fit into the expected model of a pupil with lots of energy disrupting the classroom. Some girls may be more hyperactive, or have hyperactive elements, but it may be viewed as part of their personality being bubbly rather than part of ADHD.

Girls with ADD still have challenges in a classroom environment, even if they are not so obvious. This could include:

- fidgeting;
- daydreaming;
- mis-hearing instructions.

Girls with ADD are more likely to have lower self-esteem or feel more anxious or have depression than their peers.

Strategies to support pupils with ADHD and ADD

- Establish rules and routines.
- Extra time on tests.
- Instruction and assignments tailored to the child.
- Frequent positive reinforcement and feedback.
- Offer choices.
- Using technology to assist with tasks.
- The use of a note-taker or scribe to capture ideas.
- Use visual reminders.
- Hands-on learning.
- Allowing movement breaks.
- Use active class participation frequently.
- Changes to the environment to limit distraction.
- Extra help with staying organised.

PROFESSIONAL DISCUSSION

Have you identified any pupils with ADHD/ADD in your host class?

- What has been your experience of managing their emotions and behaviour?
- Have you found this challenging?

Take the opportunity to discuss this pupil with your mentor.

- What strategies do they find are effective for the pupil and for them to implement?

Try out some of these strategies and reflect on them as part of your on-going targets.

Attachment Disorder

Attachment disorders can occur if there is a disruption to the positive bonding process between a child and their primary caregivers. Attachment disorders are common with pupils that are in foster care, who are living with other family members such as grandparents, or if they are adopted. The ability to build positive relationships can be affected long term, and pupils may have issues around trust. Behaviour of pupils with attachment issues or who have been affected by traumatic events can be disruptive and unpredictable. It is a complex area of need and as a teacher you will need support from your SENCo with interventions and strategies that are tailored for the needs of your pupil. As you will recall from the earlier case study of Mateo and his grandmother Amelie, attachment can also co-occur with areas such as anxiety and the case study is very relevant to this section, too.

Your school is likely to deliver training on aspects of Adverse Childhood Experiences (ACEs) and trauma, the section below will outline key areas that you will learn about. Seek out further training from your school with this, and as you move beyond your teacher training year.

Adverse Childhood Experiences (ACEs) and Trauma

ACEs relate to combined traumatic events that have a significant impact upon a child's life. There are three types of ACE:

1 acute, which relates to a one-off incident such as the death of a pet.
2 chronic, which is when repeated experiences impact a child such as witnessing domestic violence.
3 complex, in which there is an invasive nature to the trauma such as abuse, neglect, death of a parent or a parent in prison.

Chronic or complex ACEs are more challenging to support and work through with pupils in schools, and they are more likely to have a long-lasting impact on pupils.

The effects of ACEs on pupils could include an impact on their cognitive development and learning which might present challenges in retaining information or learning new information. The pupil may develop sensory processing difficulties or there may be an impact on executive functioning which includes the skills needed for organisation of daily life tasks and school tasks. We know from research that as a result of trauma and attachment issues, a child's brain may develop differently. Pupils may have a heightened response such as hypervigilance and the fight/flight response, which again, could impact on their behaviour in the classroom. Behaviour may present similarly to pupils with ADHD, and strategies to support ADHD may also be useful for pupils with attachment and trauma. The pupil may have delays or issues with social and communication development, impacting upon their relationships with their peers. Alongside this, there may be language delay and the need for support and intervention from a speech and language therapist. As pupils get older, they may become involved in drug and alcohol misuse.

Pupils will need support in the following ways:

- To develop resilience to recover from stressful situations.
- To be supported by loving families.
- To be supported by a safe community.
- To be embraced by a welcoming atmosphere.
- If consequences are needed, they should be logical.
- Repair relationships swiftly.
- Prepare pupils for any changes in routine.

As you will see, there are overlaps in terms of effects and strategies to support other SEND areas of need.

Activity

Go back to the case study of Mateo and his grandmother Amelie. Consider the areas of attachment that may affect Mateo, and how these may present as challenges within your own classroom.

Note down some strategies that would be useful to support Mateo in class.

Discuss these strategies with your peers, can they suggest additional strategies that would be useful?

Communication and Behaviour

Communication and behaviour can be disrupted across all areas of SEMH. It is important to look at the underlying needs of your pupil and what is causing this disruption.

This is why we have moved away from using terms such as Behavioural Disorders which were used in the past frameworks for SEND.

SEMH needs may present as behavioural challenges or disruptions and difficulty with learning, but understanding what lies beneath the observable behaviour is vital in understanding your pupils' needs and supporting them to lead a fulfilling and happy life both in and out of school.

By identifying SEMH needs early, this can prevent escalation of the need, and subsequent behaviours. This can be done through creating an inclusive and supportive environment where your pupils feel safe and secure to make mistakes.

Strategies to support pupils

Some further general strategies to support pupils' overall well-being and SEMH needs and behaviour in your class could include:

- Ensure that you know and understand your pupils' strengths and difficulties.
- Follow any plans and targets that have been set by educational professionals such as an educational psychologist.
- Provide opportunities for pupils to recognise and develop their strengths.
- Build in activities that pupils enjoy.
- Identify what is going well and celebrate this.
- Ask how a pupil is feeling rather than make assumptions, as they may be feeling differently to what you anticipate, and this will help to identify what is going on for them.
- Build resilience and normalise failure; change the use of your language so that you say, 'you can't do that yet' and celebrate when they achieve it.
- Support the development of independence.
- Use active listening.
- Support pupils to recognise, name and describe feelings, developing to describing the range and intensity of feelings and emotions of themselves and others.
- Strategies for managing feelings.
- Support pupils to understand how their behaviour affects other people.
- Support pupils to recognise what affects positively and negatively their own mental health.
- Support pupils to motivate themselves and pick themselves up after failing at something.
- Support pupils to understand how they feel about change and transitions and how to cope with these.
- Support pupils to understand the consequences of discrimination and bullying and how to ask for help if they become victims of this.
- Offer and use emotional consistency.
- Use language positively; focus on behaviour you want to see rather than what you don't want from your pupil.
- If a pupil is reluctant to engage with you, see if they will engage and build a relationship with another member of staff.

- Ensure that the classroom environment is as calm and relaxed as possible.
- Host a well-being week with a whole school focus.
- Put up school displays promoting positive mental health.
- Build nurture groups.
- Host mental health breakfasts.
- Develop resilience training.

You could also practise with your pupils recognising and expressing their emotions and feelings. When a pupil is appearing to be overwhelmed or aggressive, try starting a calm conversation with them so that you can both understand how they are feeling. You could use conversation starters such as:

- I wonder if...
- Maybe we can....
- Let's try....

Distracting and re-engaging them positively can de-escalate the behaviour and begin to help you both understand what is happening for the pupil. Remember, when a pupil is feeling like this, avoid reacting and being drawn into arguments which are likely to escalate the situation further.

Chapter Summary

This chapter has looked at the third broad area of need as defined in the Code of Practice (2015): Social, Emotional and Mental Health (SEMH). There have been three main focus areas to this chapter: Mental Health Difficulties; Attention Deficit Hyperactivity Disorder (ADHD); and Attachment Disorder. Each section has given an overview of the area, what it may look like and how it may present for a pupil in your class, and then each section gives some key supporting strategies for pupils including what should be ordinarily available to them. The case study of Mateo and his grandmother Amelie gave you the opportunity to consider areas of anxiety and attachment that may affect a pupil. The final section of the chapter, Communication and behaviour, focused on the additional supporting strategies across the breadth of SEMH needs.

The DfE are working to provide materials and resources to support pupil mental health, and the link to these is in the further reading section of this chapter.

Glossary of Key Terms

- Co-occurrence – When there is more than one area of need.

Further Reading

- Anxiety UK. https://www.anxietyuk.org.uk/
- Attention Deficit Hyperactivity Disorder (ADHD) Foundation. https://www.adhdfoundation.org.uk/
- Bomber, L. (2007). *Inside I'm Hurting*. Broadway: Worth Publishing.
- Cairns, K. and Cairns, B. (2016). *Attachment, Trauma and Resilience*. London: CoramBAAF.
- Department for Education (DfE) (2021). Mental Health Well-being Resources for Teachers and Teaching Staff. https://assets.publishing.service.gov.uk/government/uploads/system/uploads/attachment_data/file/993669/Mental_Health_Resources_for_teachers_and_teaching_staff_June_2021.pdf
- Department for Education (DfE) (2023). Promoting and Supporting Mental Health and Well-being in Schools and Colleges. https://www.gov.uk/guidance/mental-health-and-wellbeing-support-in-schools-and-colleges
- Education Endowment Foundation (EEF) (2021). Special Educational Needs in Mainstream Schools; Guidance Report. https://d2tic4wvo1iusb.cloudfront.net/production/eef-guidance-reports/send/EEF_Special_Educational_Needs_in_Mainstream_Schools_Guidance_Report.pdf?v=1690614961
- Geddes, H. (2006). *Attachment in the Classroom: A Practical Guide for Schools*. Broadway: Worth Publishing.
- OCD Youth. https://ocdyouth.org/

Links to the Teachers' Standards

- *1. Set high expectations which inspire, motivate and challenge pupils*; establish a safe and stimulating environment for pupils, rooted in mutual respect.
- *2. Promote good progress and outcomes by pupils*; be aware of pupils' capabilities and their prior knowledge, and plan teaching to build on these; demonstrate knowledge and understanding of how pupils learn and how this impacts on teaching
- *5. Adapt teaching to respond to the strengths and needs of all pupils*; have a secure understanding of how a range of factors can inhibit pupils' ability to learn, and how best to overcome these; have a clear understanding of the needs of all pupils, including those with special educational needs; those of high ability; those with English as an additional language; those with disabilities; and be able to use and evaluate distinctive teaching approaches to engage and support them.
- *7. Manage behaviour effectively to ensure a good and safe learning environment*; have clear rules and routines for behaviour in classrooms, and take responsibility for promoting good and courteous behaviour both in classrooms and around the school, in accordance with the school's behaviour policy.
- *8. Fulfil wider professional responsibilities*; take responsibility for improving teaching through appropriate professional development, responding to advice and feedback from colleagues.

References

Alix, S. (2023). *The Neurodiversity Handbook for Trainee Teachers*. London: Sage.

Department of Education and Department of Health (2015). Special Educational Needs and Disability Code of Practice: 0 to 25 years. Statutory guidance for organisations which work with and support children and young people who have special educational needs or disabilities. Government Publications.

Department for Education (DfE) (2023). Promoting and Supporting Mental Health and Well-being in Schools and Colleges. https://www.gov.uk/guidance/mental-health-and-wellbeing-support-in-schools-and-colleges

6

Sensory and Physical Needs

Chapter Aims

- To gain an overview of the fourth broad area of need within the Code of Practice – Sensory and physical needs.
- To gain detailed knowledge and explanation of Vision Impairment (VI), Hearing Impairment (HI), Multi-Sensory Impairment (MSI), Physical Disability (PD) and sensory needs linked to current research and theory.
- To develop an understanding of Vision Impairment (VI).
- To develop an understanding of Hearing Impairment (HI).
- To develop an understanding of Multi-Sensory Impairment (MSI).
- To develop an understanding of Physical Disability (PD).
- To develop an understanding of sensory needs.
- To gain an understanding of some supporting strategies for pupils with sensory and physical needs.

Links to the Core Content Framework (CCF)

Adaptive Teaching

- ***Learn that*** adapting teaching in a responsive way, including by providing targeted support to pupils who are struggling, is likely to increase pupil success.
- ***Learn that*** pupils with special educational needs or disabilities are likely to require additional or adapted support; working closely with colleagues, families and pupils to understand barriers and identify effective strategies is essential.
- ***Learn how to*** observe how expert colleagues adapt lessons, whilst maintaining high expectations for all, so that all pupils have the opportunity to meet expectations and deconstructing this approach.

Professional Behaviours

- ***Learn how to*** strengthen pedagogical and subject knowledge by participating in wider networks.
- ***Learn how to*** receive clear, consistent and effective mentoring in how to work closely with the SENCo and other professionals supporting pupils with additional needs, including how to make explicit links between interventions delivered outside of lessons with classroom teaching.

Introduction

In this final chapter of Part II, we look at what we mean by 'Sensory and Physical Needs' when it relates to the Code of Practice.

Sensory and physical needs is the fourth broad area of need within the Code of Practice (2015). This area relates to pupils that may be experiencing some form of Vision Impairment (VI), Hearing Impairment (HI), Multi-Sensory Impairment (MSI) or Physical Disability (PD).

The Code of Practice (2015) states 'Some children and young people require special educational provision because they have a disability which prevents or hinders them from making use of the educational facilities generally provided. These difficulties can be age related and may fluctuate over time. Many children and young people with vision impairment (VI), hearing impairment (HI) or a multi-sensory impairment (MSI) will require specialist support and/or equipment to access their learning, or habilitation support.' And 'Some children and young people with a physical disability (PD) require additional ongoing support and equipment to access all the opportunities available to their peers.'

The final section of this chapter will examine sensory needs in further detail, which can co-occur in pupils with sensory impairments such as hearing and visual loss, as well as being a stand-alone condition or co-occurring with other conditions such as autism and ADHD.

Vision Impairment (VI)

A vision impairment is when there is a loss of sight that cannot be corrected with glasses or contact lenses. There are two main types of visual impairment:

1. When someone is registered as being partially sighted and the level of sight impairment is classed as moderate.
2. When the person is registered as being blind, and there is a severe sight impairment and activities that rely on sight are impossible.

When considering the education of vision impaired pupils, it is important to understand that pupils should have fair access to the school curriculum, and that they have opportunities to develop their independence as a learner and social inclusion in preparation for independent living and employment, which is recommended in the Code of Practice (2015).

Strategies to support pupils with a visual impairment include

- Providing a variety of hands-on, meaningful experiences through real-world experiences in which your pupil can have a direct understanding of something and not just a verbal explanation.
- Talking about these experiences with your pupil beforehand, as well as while the experience is happening.
- Use words to label objects, people, and experiences that are appropriate to the pupil's developmental level.
- Offer opportunities for the pupil to explore and interact with a wide range of materials and real objects. This helps to compare size, shape, texture and other attributes, while also supporting the pupil to develop basic concepts and an understanding of same and different.
- Encourage daily purposeful, fun movement activities to build gross motor and fine motor abilities. This will support the use of object and tactile symbols or braille.
- Support the pupil to interact with others in safe and comfortable environments.
- Create a literacy-rich environment, in which the pupil is aware that others are reading and writing.
- Provide accessible labels in the environment on the pupil's chair, table and equipment. These should be in the pupil's preferred format (large print, braille, objects, tactile symbols).
- Read aloud using stories and books that are interesting and appropriate for your pupil.
- Use real objects and personal experiences to increase understanding.
- Determine what medium is best for an individual pupil. This may be braille, print, dual media, auditory strategies, objects, symbols, or some combination.

- Provide books and literacy tools in a format that is accessible to your pupil.
- Make sure the classroom is well organised and labelled, with good acoustics. Keep background noise to a minimum.
- Consider your seating arrangements for your pupil to ensure access to the interactive whiteboard, the flipchart and any demonstrations. Pupils should be seated with their back to the window so that shadows are not cast over their work.
- Check lighting levels to make sure there's appropriate and comfortable light for the pupil, including use of blinds.
- Highlight steps and features within the school and playgrounds or outside space.
- Carry out an environmental audit as advised by and with your SENCo and Local Authority (LA) advisor, in liaison with a Qualified Teacher for the Visually Impaired (QTVI).
- PowerPoints should have clearly numbered slides, so that pupils using personal copies of the presentation can easily follow in the lesson.
- Give clear verbal explanations when giving a demonstration. Verbalise what you write on a board.
- Say the pupil's name before talking to them so they know who you're directing the request or instruction to. Remember that children and young people with a VI are unlikely to follow non-verbal communication.
- Do not stand against a window, as your face becomes difficult to see.

Encourage pupils to:

- Use aids such as example writing slopes, glass or hand magnifiers.
- Keep glasses clean, if applicable, as advised by QTVI.
- Provide rest periods or alternate activities to reduce visual effort. For example, use audio books or a practical activity. Reduce unnecessary visual information from materials or copying from the board.
- Consider arrangements for break and lunchtime activities.
- Use a classroom tablet computer to take photos and enlarge images to help with access.
- Consider access to assemblies.
- Give the pupil their own copies of materials or a laptop or tablet displaying information.

It is important to work collaboratively with other practitioners as there may be several supporting your pupil. Ensure that you get to know your pupil individually as a learner, and how their visual impairment impacts upon their learning.

Hearing Impairment (HI)

A pupil's hearing loss could be mild, moderate, moderately severe, severe or profound and it can be one or both ears.

There are four main types of hearing impairment that you could be presented with in pupils within your class:

- Sensorineural hearing loss – when a pupil has hearing loss due to the inner ear (cochlea) or acoustic nerve. Damage to these structures can occur due to exposure to loud noises, illness (meningitis), ototoxic medications, or genetics. Sensorineural hearing loss is permanent, and treatments include the use of hearing aids and cochlear implants.
- Conductive hearing loss – is when something prevents sound from passing through the outer or middle ear and into the inner ear. This can occur when earwax or fluid builds up in the ear canal, or when there is damage to the eardrum or bones in the middle ear. It may also be due to a birth defect that prevents sound waves from entering the ear to stimulate the acoustic nerve. Treatments may include surgery to repair structural abnormalities, a procedure to remove blockages, or the implementation of a hearing aid, cochlear implant or bone-anchored hearing aid.
- Mixed hearing loss – a pupil may have both a sensorineural and conductive hearing loss which is classified as a mixed hearing loss. Mixed hearing loss affects both the inner ear and outer or middle ear, and can lead to a more profound hearing loss. Treatments will vary depending on the severity of the hearing loss, but in addition to a surgical procedure, hearing aids and cochlear implants may be necessary.
- Auditory Neuropathy Spectrum Disorder (ANSD) – sound is able to enter an ear normally and reach the acoustic nerve, but there is an issue when the sound is transmitted to the brain. This can happen due to the hair cells of the inner ear being damaged and they are unable to properly transmit sound information to the brain. Sometimes a genetic mutation is the cause of this hearing loss, and other times damage that occurs to the auditory nerve can lead to ANSD. Pupils with ANSD may seem to have normal hearing sensitivity on a hearing test, but they may struggle to understand spoken words. In some cases, a hearing aid or cochlear implant paired with a hearing assistive technology (HAT) system can help mitigate the negative effects of this hearing loss. However, more severe cases, in which the person has great difficulty understanding speech, may require the use of a visual communication technique, like sign language or a picture exchange communication system (PECS).

Signs that a pupil has hearing loss include:

- has limited or unclear speech;
- does not following directions;
- appears to be not paying attention;
- hears only parts of a conversation and asks for information to be repeated;
- is not able to hear everyday sounds, like a school bell;
- has learning difficulties;
- does not respond when their name is called;
- has problems with concentration, excessive tiredness and frustration with work that starts to affect their behaviour;

- watches your lips intently as you speak;
- speaks too loudly or too quietly;
- watches others do something before attempting it themselves;
- becomes increasingly withdrawn from others in the classroom;
- there is delayed speech and communication development;
- mishears or mispronounces words;
- is not able to hear what's happening if there is any background noise;
- makes minimal contributions to classroom discussions;
- has difficulty with reading and linking it to speech.

Strategies to support pupils with hearing loss

- **Make seating changes.** Pupils with hearing loss may need to sit closer to the front of the class to read lips, or hear more clearly. Also consider arranging chairs in your classroom in a U-shape or circle so that pupils with hearing loss can better interact with classmates.
- **Minimise background noise when possible.** This may mean finding quiet areas for a pupil to work.
- **Use an FM system.** This device helps a pupil with hearing loss hear their teachers better in a noisy classroom. To use the system, a teacher wears a microphone/transmitter and the pupil wears the receiver, which amplifies sound.
- **Face pupils when you speak.** Most pupils with hearing loss can speech read to some extent. To help them, face them when you talk, talk slowly and clearly, and don't shout. As long as they have their device on, you can speak in a normal tone.
- **Use lots of pictures, graphics, and text labels.** Many pupils with hearing loss are supported by visuals.
- **Use technology to make learning easier.**
- **Encourage participation** in classroom activities, physical education, and extra-curricular activities.

A pupil with a hearing impairment may withdraw from others and their education. There may be frustration of not being able to express themselves or communicate fully how they would like to, and they may not feel as though they are being heard. This frustration can damage relationships and their progress in education.

CASE STUDY

From a class teacher.

Huang is in Year 3 in primary school. She has a conductive hearing loss which is considered moderate because she cannot hear clearly. It is permanent rather than temporary. Huang's language and speech skills are delayed, likely due to her not hearing adequately

(Continued)

in early childhood. Huang uses hearing aids and has regular appointments with an audiologist who ensures her devices are working correctly.

The SENCo and I work together with her parents and health support services to develop a plan of strategies on how to support Huang in the classroom. These strategies include:

- Instructional Content – Huang is given repeated opportunities to read aloud to help build fluency.
- Instructional Procedures – As Huang has a mild to moderate hearing impairment, we focus on both oral and auditory approaches to help her develop a wide variety of skills that will help her communicate in the classroom.
- Instructional Environment – Huang is placed in a seat close to me and the use of visuals is used more frequently.
- Instructional Technology – Huang uses hearing aids and a loop system that isolates my speech and transmits it directly to the hearing aid, making the teacher's speech more intelligible to the her – it took me a little while to get used to this, remembering to turn it on, and that it was on when I went to do other things outside of the classroom.

Huang is encouraged to speak aloud in class and participate in classroom discussion, her lessons are hands on and visual so that she can use her proficient senses to help supplement her impaired one. I have very high expectations for Huang, and we need to work together to ensure that she reaches her potential. Collaboration between the school, external educational and health professionals and Huang's parents are key to her making the progress in school that she is able to.

Multi-Sensory Impairment (MSI)

A multi-sensory impairment means that a pupil has impairments in both their vision and their hearing. These sensory losses can range from mild to profound and they can co-occur with additional learning needs, other diagnosis and medical needs. In addition, many pupils with MSI have impairments of other senses, as well as with their sight and hearing. They may have poor balance, limited movement, an impaired sense of smell or they may be hyper- or hypo-sensitive to touch. Pupils with MSI need to get as much information as possible from any useful sight and hearing they have and from their other senses. Some pupils with MSI become very skilled in using their other senses such as using touch as a way of communicating and learning about their environment, or their sense of smell to identify people and places.

Supporting strategies would be similar to those for pupils with a VI or HI, with additional consideration of the impairment of both senses.

Your Local Authority (LA) is a good place to start when seeking support or advice; they should have a specialist teacher for MSI who can advise on personalised strategies and support for your multi-sensory impaired pupil.

Physical Disability (PD)

A physical disability is when you have a physical or mental impairment which is defined as a 'limitation on a person's physical functioning, mobility, dexterity or stamina' that has a 'substantial' and 'long-term' negative effect on your ability to do normal daily activities (Equality Act, 2010).

In this context, substantial means more than minor or trivial. For example, it would take much longer for someone to complete a daily task such as getting dressed. Long term means that it is occurring for twelve months or more.

A physical disability could include:

- Acquired brain injury
- Arthritis
- Cerebral palsy
- Chromosome disorders
- Muscular dystrophy
- Spina bifida

Supporting strategies for a pupil with a physical disability will be very personalised towards their individual needs. There are general strategies though that will be useful for all your PD pupils, some of these will be set up and reviewed with your SENCo or LA advisor.

Strategies to support pupils with a physical disability

Encourage independence.

- Remove obstacles so that your pupil can move freely during lessons.
- Encourage support for the pupil from other class members.
- Consider physical access issues such as ramps, toilets, lifts and classroom layout.
- Incorporate advice from the educational professionals such as the occupational therapist.
- Specialised equipment may also be necessary such as adapted keyboards or special desks.
- If writing is difficult consider using a scribe or recording device.
- Allow pupils extra time to complete tasks.
- If teaching Physical Education, note that slower-paced activities are better than those requiring a fast response.
- Pupils may have low self-image; therefore, it is important to ensure that the pupil feels included and is encouraged and praised.
- If your pupil uses a wheelchair, place yourself at their eye level when talking to them.
- The height of the board in the classroom may have to be lowered if your pupil is in a wheelchair.

PROFESSIONAL DISCUSSION

Arrange a meeting with your SENCo. Discuss what range of physical disabilities they have supported as a SENCo, and consider the following questions:

- What challenges have they found the most difficult?
- What successes have they had?
- What made them successful?
- What was the impact on the pupils?

Sensory Needs; Sensory Processing Difficulties

Sensory Processing Disorder (SPD)

SPD was introduced in Chapter 3 when discussing the section on autism. This chapter is going to take a more in-depth look into this area. As mentioned earlier, there can be crossovers between the broad areas of need, and this is an area where this can be seen.

Reflect

Recall what you already know about sensory processing, and what you may have learnt in Chapter 3. Refer back to any notes to refresh your memory and build on your existing knowledge when working through the next section.

Sensory processing is a neurological process in which information is taken in through our senses and then organised so that we can respond to it appropriately. We do this through smell, taste, touch, sound, vision, movement and gravity and body position. Most pupils use this information automatically and effectively, but for pupils with SPD this can affect their daily lives including their behaviour, social interaction, education and work (Alix, 2023). This can include normal daily tasks such as brushing your teeth, having your hair cut, having a shower, going into a shop, eating a range of food with different tastes and textures, and moving around.

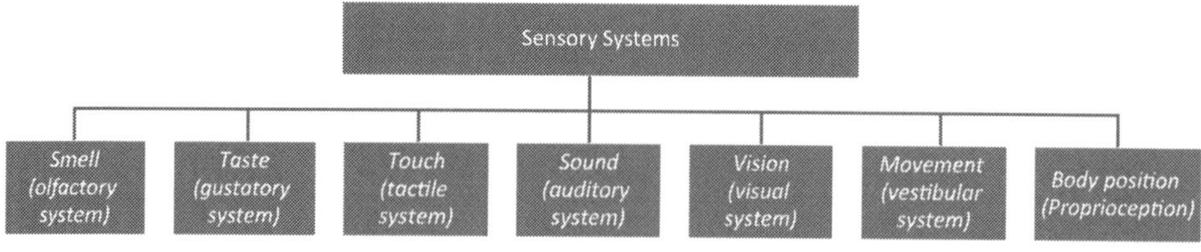

Figure 6.1 The sensory systems.

Sensory processing is the way in which our brain sorts out the sensory information that comes to us from the environment so that we can understand what is happening and manage everyday life. Our senses help us to understand and respond to what is going on around us, become alert of any dangers and support us to remain on task.

There are two main types of sensory difficulties. First, hyper (over) sensitive and includes:

- the fear of heights;
- avoidance of food textures, colours, and temperature;
- avoidance of play equipment;
- the fear of loud or sudden sounds, or an extreme response to this;
- being distracted by background noises;
- disliking touch such as hair brushing or washing, the shower and having nails cut.

The second is hypo (under) sensitive and includes:

- appearing not to feel pain to temperature;
- seeking out movement such as rocking or fidgeting;
- chewing things;
- having poor awareness of the surrounding environment;
- having the need to touch people or seek out hugs;
- being fidgety and unable to sit still;
- likes spinning and jumping.

At times, depending on the environment and situation, both hyper and hypo can be interchangeable within an individual. SPD often co-occurs with Autism and ADHD but can also be a stand-alone disorder or co-occur with a pupil with other sensory disabilities such as a visual or hearing loss.

In a school and classroom environment where there are a range of noises and smells, this can be difficult. Let's take each area in turn and think about what the impact might be for each area and what considerations and strategies might be useful.

Activity

As you work through the following explanations of each of the sensory systems, take a few moments to stop and bring to your consciousness that sensory system and 'feel' what it is like for you.

- How does it help you to understand your current environment?
- How might it feel if it wasn't working in the way that it currently is?

Smell (olfactory system)

Pupils may be distracted by different scents which could include perfume or aftershaves, cooking smells, or the musty smell of an old building. Smells to someone with SPD can appear much more intense and can be distracting or an irritant that can affect focus. Some people with SPD can seek out strong scents, wanting to inhale scents like detergents on clothes. Small children might put objects up their noses or smell toys before playing with them.

- Consider changing strong perfumes and scents for something lighter or more natural.
- Consider your distance from pupils when needed, particularly after coffee breaks and lunch when you may have remnants of your breaks on your person which pupils may not like.
- Set up scent seeking activities for younger pupils so that they can gain sensory seeking input.

Taste (gustatory system)

Your pupils could possibly have sensitivity to taste and textures which may limit their food choices. They may prefer to have the same food over and over again which is a safe taste and texture to them. They may want their foods separately and not like them to be mixed. They may also lick objects or people.

- Tasting sessions are a good idea to introduce new foods, not overloading a child, and being mindful of what is on offer at lunch and snack times.
- Pupils may need to bring in food from home during these times, rather than having what is on offer from the school.
- Chewy toys also help the sensory aspects of needing something in the mouth and are often helpful for younger pupils.

Touch (tactile system)

Pupils may be hyper or hypo sensitive to touch. It could be that the pupil doesn't want, or like unwanted touch by others. You may see them physically flinch or step away from the slightest of touches. At other times, the pupil may seek out touch, and want to be hugged or squeezed very tightly.

- Use a no-pressure approach, do not make a child hold hands with others or play games that include the need for physical touch.

- The use of pressure toys can be very useful to alleviate the need for hugs and squeezes; items such as large yoga balls, or weighted blankets can easily be incorporated in early years or primary settings.
- Heavy rucksacks can be beneficial for secondary aged pupils, and some are made with additional straps to create a tighter feeling across the chest and back.

Sound (auditory system)

Sound is a key area in the classroom that can be distracting for pupils with SPD. Pupils may hear very small sounds more easily. Things such as a tap dripping in the background, or a clock ticking can sound thunderous to pupils with SPD. The disturbance from other groups' conversations can have a profound impact on concentration and focus. Consider your classroom environment, how might the noise levels impact on your pupils?

- Monitor noise levels in class and consider the use of noise cancelling headphones for your SPD pupils during activity work.
- Pupils may also become distressed by loud, sudden noises, such as a balloon popping or a hand dryer in the toilets. This may cause a high level of stress or anxiety and the pupil may need additional time to regulate from this.

Vision (visual system)

A pupil may stare at artificial lighting, or avoid it for a preference of natural light. They may hold objects close to their face so that they can filter out any distractions. They may become excited by flashing lights or spinning toys.

- Offer sensory rooms and experiences where possible, some schools may already have these areas set up.
- Give your pupils the time and opportunity to take breaks and explore sensory experiences as part of their day.
- Think about where a pupil is positioned in the classroom, are they near natural or artificial lighting? What sensory input do they need for this lesson? This may change throughout the day, particularly as pupils begin to tire, they may seek sensory input.

Movement (vestibular system)

This system relates to balance and movement in space and relative to gravity. Signs that a pupil is having difficulty with their vestibular system would be them experiencing dizziness, spatial disorientation, visual disturbances, motion sickness and headaches. A pupil may seek out movement such as spinning, rocking, or climbing. Stimming is a normal movement for pupils with SPD and it should not be stopped.

- Give opportunities throughout the day for the pupil to experience forms of movement such as swinging and climbing.
- Offer the use of fidget toys.

Gravity

SPD may cause gravitational insecurity, which affects balance and the ability to process vestibular stimulation as outlined above. The pupil may be fearful of, or avoid certain physical activities, have a fear of heights or large rides, escalators, or lifts. They may have a resistance to being upside down, so this may affect PE lessons in which pupils are doing gym or using climbing equipment.

- Give regular sensory breaks throughout the day.
- Look for signs in your pupils that indicate they may need a sensory break or change.

Body position (proprioception)

This is the sense of where your body is, your awareness of joints and muscles, the location and orientation of them in relation to other parts of the body. Pupils may have an unusual walking gait, they may like to sit in a position that is not seen as ideal in the classroom such as slouching or tucking their legs underneath them. It can impact through clumsiness, or for example throwing a ball too hard.

- Consider the chair the pupil is on; can they make themselves comfortable so that they can engage with the learning?

PROFESSIONAL DISCUSSION

Arrange a discussion with the SENCo.

Consider a pupil with a hearing impairment, visual impairment, or multi-sensory impairment.

- How has this affected the other areas of their sensory systems?
- What have they noticed?
- What additional strategies were put into place for these pupils?
- What was effective?

Chapter Summary

This chapter has looked at the fourth broad area of need as defined in the Code of Practice (2015): Sensory and Physical needs. There have been five focus areas to this chapter: Vision Impairment (VI); Hearing Impairment (HI); Multi-Sensory Impairment (MSI); Physical Disability (PD); and Sensory Needs; Sensory Processing Difficulties. Each section has given an overview of the area, what it may look like and how it may present for a pupil in your class, and then each section gives some key supporting strategies for pupils including what should be available to them. You have reflected upon your own sensory systems, and you can now consider applying some new strategies in the classroom for your pupils.

Glossary of Key Terms

- Auditory Neuropathy Spectrum Disorder (ANSD) – When sound is able to enter an ear normally and reach the acoustic nerve, but there is an issue when the sound is transmitted to the brain.
- Conductive hearing loss – When something prevents sound from passing through the outer or middle ear and into the inner ear.
- Hearing Impairment (HI) – Hearing loss could be mild, moderate, moderately severe, severe or profound and it can be one or both ears.
- Mixed hearing loss – When there is both a sensorineural and conductive hearing loss.
- Multi-Sensory Impairment (MSI) – When there are impairments in both vision and their hearing.
- Physical Disability (PD) – When you have a physical or mental impairment which limits physical functioning, mobility, dexterity or stamina that has a 'substantial' and 'long-term' negative effect.
- Sensorineural hearing loss – A hearing loss due to the inner ear (cochlea) or acoustic nerve.
- Sensory Processing Difficulty – When the brain finds it difficult to sort out the sensory information that comes in, and results in hyper or hypo sensitivity.
- Vision Impairment (VI) – When there is a loss of sight that cannot be corrected with glasses or contact lenses.

Further Reading

- British Sign. https://www.british-sign.co.uk/
- The Makaton Charity. https://www.makaton.org/
- National Deaf Children's Society. https://www.ndcs.org.uk/

- National Deaf Children's Society. Deaf Friendly Teaching; for Primary School Staff. https://www.ndcs.org.uk/documents-and-resources/deaf-friendly-teaching-for-primary-school-staff/
- NHS hearing loss. https://www.nhs.uk/conditions/hearing-loss/symptoms/
- Physical Disability; PDnet. https://pdnet.org.uk/
- RNIB Education and Learning. https://www.rnib.org.uk/your-eyes/navigating-sight-loss/education-and-learning/
- RNIB How your child will be supported in a mainstream school. https://www.rnib.org.uk/living-with-sight-loss/supporting-others/parenting-a-child-with-a-vision-impairment/how-your-child-will-be-supported-in-a-mainstream-school/
- Sense. https://www.sense.org.uk/
- Sensory Processing Disorder UK. https://thesensoryseeker.com/sensory-processing-disorder-in-the-uk/
- Shine Charity, Physical disability and educational settings. https://www.shinecharity.org.uk/for-professionals/faqs-about-physical-disability-and-educational-settings

Links to the Teachers' Standards

- *1. Set high expectations which inspire, motivate and challenge pupils*; establish a safe and stimulating environment for pupils, rooted in mutual respect.
- *2. Promote good progress and outcomes by pupils*; be aware of pupils' capabilities and their prior knowledge, and plan teaching to build on these; demonstrate knowledge and understanding of how pupils learn and how this impacts on teaching
- *5. Adapt teaching to respond to the strengths and needs of all pupils*; have a secure understanding of how a range of factors can inhibit pupils' ability to learn, and how best to overcome these; have a clear understanding of the needs of all pupils, including those with special educational needs; those of high ability; those with English as an additional language; those with disabilities; and be able to use and evaluate distinctive teaching approaches to engage and support them.
- *8. Fulfil wider professional responsibilities*; take responsibility for improving teaching through appropriate professional development, responding to advice and feedback from colleagues.

References

Alix, S. (2023). *The Neurodiversity Handbook for Trainee Teachers*. London: Sage.

Department of Education and Department of Health (2015). Special Educational Needs and Disability Code of Practice: 0 to 25 Years. Statutory guidance for organisations which work with and support children and young people who have special educational needs or disabilities. Government Publications.

Government. Equality Act 2010. https://www.legislation.gov.uk/ukpga/2010/15/contents

Part III

Developing Classroom Practice

7

Working with Support Staff, Educational Professionals and Parents

Chapter Aims

- To gain an understanding of how to work with Teaching Assistants (TAs) and Learning Support Assistants (LSAs) effectively when supporting SEND pupils, which is rooted in evidence-based practice and research.
- To have an overview of the different roles in education that might work together to support SEND pupils.
- To consider approaches to working with parents and carers of SEND pupils, and consider their perspectives and concerns.
- To understand how collaborative working is key in supporting SEND pupils.

Links to the Core Content Framework (CCF)

High Expectations

- ***Learn that*** a culture of mutual trust and respect supports effective relationships.
- ***Learn how to*** seek opportunities to engage parents and carers in the education of their children (e.g. proactively highlighting successes) with support from expert colleagues to understand how this engagement changes depending on the age and development stage of the pupil.

Adaptive Teaching

- ***Learn that*** pupils with special educational needs or disabilities are likely to require additional or adapted support; working closely with colleagues, families and pupils to understand barriers and identify effective strategies is essential.
- ***Learn how to*** make effective use of teaching assistants and other adults in the classroom under supervision of expert colleagues.

Professional Behaviours

- ***Learn that*** effective professional development is likely to be sustained over time, involve expert support or coaching and opportunities for collaboration.
- ***Learn that*** building effective relationships with parents, carers and families can improve pupils' motivation, behaviour and academic success.
- ***Learn that*** Teaching Assistants (TAs) can support pupils more effectively when they are prepared for lessons by teachers, and when TAs supplement rather than replace support from teachers.
- ***Learn that*** SENCos, pastoral leaders, careers advisors and other specialist colleagues also have valuable expertise and can ensure that appropriate support is in place for pupils.
- ***Learn how to*** discuss and analyse with expert colleagues how experienced colleagues seek ways to support individual colleagues and working as part of a team.
- ***Learn how to*** observe how expert colleagues communicate with parents and carers proactively and make effective use of parents' evenings to engage parents and carers in their children's schooling and deconstructing this approach.
- ***Learn how to*** prepare teaching assistants for lessons under supervision of expert colleagues.

Introduction

Part III of this book takes what you have learnt so far about SEND and the broad areas of need, and begins to consider further applying these skills, and putting them into practice alongside learning new information and strategies, such as working collaboratively and assessing pupils using the graduated approach.

This chapter focuses on collaborative working, working with your support staff (Teaching Assistants (TAs) and Learning Support Assistants (LSAs)), wider educational professionals, and parents and carers.

Working with Teaching Assistants and Learning Support Assistants

In a primary school, it is likely that if you have SEND pupils in your class, that you will also have a TA or LSA working with you for either part of the day, or all of the day.

So, what is their role?

Reflect

Think about your teacher training classroom.

- Do you work with a TA/LSA?
- Do you have the same one, or more?
- Are they there within your class all of the time?
- What role do you think they have?
- How does your mentor direct them?
- What sort of jobs or teaching and learning do they do?

If it's possible, discuss this with some of your teacher training colleagues. You may find that there will be differences in roles and expectations from school to school. We will discuss why this is now.

Let's start by outlining the difference between a TA and an LSA.

A TA will tend to work across the whole class offering academic support to all pupils and being a good role model to them, they are directed by the class teacher to work with different groups depending on the focus.

An LSA will more often work one-to-one with pupils, they may also have a pastoral role, and they may support or lead on the implementation and conducting of specific interventions.

There are many similarities between the two roles, and often the terms of the two roles will be used interchangeably. The role definition will depend upon the contract of the support worker, and therefore the role that the TA or LSA will be undertaking in your individual school. It is always best to find out what this is, and what the expectations are for the role in your own host school, so that you know the type of work you should be directing your TA/LSA to be doing.

It is likely that as a class teacher you won't be line managing your LSA/TA, that is normally carried out by the SENCo, or a head of inclusion or pastoral care or someone that is part of the senior leadership group. However, you will be directing the work that they do within the classroom to support your pupils, so you will need to develop your working relationship with them and take on leadership qualities to do this effectively.

Webster, Blatchford, and Russell (2013) carried out some research in relation to the use of TAs specifically. They looked at the effectiveness of the use of TAs, how they were deployed, and the sort of tasks they were doing. They concluded that when TAs were trained to deliver specific intervention programmes, this worked well, but when TAs taught classes, this was not effective. So, there was support for highly focused intervention programmes for pupils delivered by TAs, but there was also a very clear message that TAs should not be teaching whole classes (they haven't been trained for this). However, there are many other aspects that TAs and LSAs are responsible for within the classroom, so what about these?

The Education Endowment Foundation (2018) reviewed the research around the use of TAs and agreed with Webster, Blatchford, and Russell (2013) that there were positives and negatives around how they were being used. They stated that the current model did not support pupil progress effectively and could even be detrimental to pupils if they became reliant on support and developed a dependency on a one-to-one TA. However, positives were seen in many areas, such as TAs supporting motivation, confidence, and self-esteem in pupils, and they eased workload for teachers, and enabled the teacher to focus more time on the teaching (Alix, 2023b).

TAs/LSAs come to this role with a range of qualifications and experience, some with a great deal of experience (and they may make you feel like a novice in the classroom as a trainee teacher, compared to their own experience), and others will be new to education altogether. There can also be little training and induction for TAs/LSAs, with time short in the day, and a lack of money for training. You will need to consider your role in directing and supporting them in the classroom, to ensure that pupils are in turn supported to make the progress that they can.

The EEF (2018) outline seven recommendations of how best TAs/LSAs should be used within schools, the link to this document is in the further reading section at the end of the chapter. There are seven recommendations:

1 TAs should not be used as an informal teaching resource for low attaining pupils.
2 Use TAs to add value to what teachers do, not replace them.
3 Use TAs to help pupils develop independent learning skills and manage their own learning.
4 Ensure TAs are fully prepared for their role in the classroom.
5 Use TAs to deliver high quality one-to-one and small group support using structured interventions.
6 Adopt evidence-based interventions to support TAs in their small group and one-to-one instruction.

7 Ensure explicit connections are made between learning from everyday classroom and teaching and structured interventions.

The Neurodiversity Handbook for Trainee Teachers (Alix, 2023a) examines these in turn in relation to working with neurodivergent pupils, including case studies, reflections, and discussions around these. This chapter in this book will take a different focus, and is going to look at some specific strategies that you can support your TA/LSA in developing when working with your SEND pupils as this will impact directly upon their developing practice and expertise as a TA/LSA. The relevant recommendations in relation to this are selected:

4. Ensure TAs are fully prepared for their role in the classroom.

It will be part of your role as the class teacher to direct the work of your TA/LSA, and give them clear direction and support. This is one of the Teachers' Standards that will need to be met at the end of your teacher training.

It is not just giving a TA/LSA a lesson plan and asking them to sit with a group, as I am sure that you have realised by now! So, what sort of things will you be expecting them to do on a daily basis to support your pupils? It might include:

- Directing them to check in on a child and set out the expectations and timetable for the day, ensuring that the pupil understands what is to follow throughout the day and what lessons will be taking place.
- Asking them to support the facilitation of the unstructured times of the day such as the transition times between lessons, break times and lunch times.
- Direct them to give hover support, when a pupil is working on a task in class, checking in with them, looking over what they are doing, where they are at, and offering encouragement and praise to keep them on track or to stay motivated. You are working towards independence (one of the previous recommendations), so the balance of this may change from lesson to lesson and over time. As a teacher you may need to model this if this is something that your TA/LSA is unfamiliar with doing.
- Demonstrate how hover support may include some taught elements when needed.
- Ensure that you share and discuss the pupil's IEP or EHCP targets, and how what you and your TA/LSA are doing is supporting them in working towards these.
- Ensure regular communication and feedback between yourself and your TA/LSA on the work that they have been supporting. Your pupil is your responsibility, not your TA's/LSA's. Communication between you and your TA/LSA is key so that informed decisions can be made around reviewing their progress, and adjusting the provision that they are receiving.

5. Use TAs to deliver high quality one-to-one and small group support using structured interventions.

As you have read from previous chapters in Part II of this book, some pupils could have language and comprehension barriers, not understand phrases being used, jokes that are made by others, or have difficulty with the construction and process of a conversation; for example, turn taking, listening, waiting, pausing for breath, using facial expressions and being polite. Each of these could lead to challenges when your TA/LSA is working with groups of pupils, and your TA/LSA may need support in developing strategies to work with your SEND pupils in this way.

Some suggestions to work with your TA/LSA on:

Create group rules or an agreement of expected behaviours for the group, this will provide some boundaries and safety points to refer to when needed. Rules could include:

- taking turns;
- listen when someone else is speaking;
- be respectful of other pupils' ideas;
- encourage and support other pupils to contribute and join in;
- take responsibility for a role within a task;
- if you want to disagree, disagree politely, and give a reason why you disagree;
- listen to feedback and act upon it.

These strategies will support you as a developing teacher, but will also be useful for you while working with your TA/LSA.

When carrying out group work:

- Consider where pupils are sitting, think about the pupils within the group and which pupils might work better with each other.
- Think about their strengths and challenges, how might you use these within the group working?
- Consider the type of task that pupils are doing, are there any pupils who will be better taking a lead role or encouraging other pupils to join in?
- Are there pupils within the group that are stronger with their reading skills or discussing ideas?
- You may want pupils to work in pairs within the group rather than all pupils contributing to the discussion or task. The TA/LSA will still be able to listen and support each of the pairs within the group.

A further overview of some possible interventions is outlined in the next section.

6. ***Adopt evidence-based interventions to support TAs in their small group and one-to one instruction.***

Working in Pairs

Working in pairs can help to develop skills in preparation for group work and has many benefits. One idea to support this development that you may have already seen being used in class is think-pair-share.

Think-Pair-Share is a strategy that is designed to encourage student involvement. First, participants listen to the teacher's question. Then they think of a response. They pair up with someone and discuss their responses. Finally, they are asked to share their responses with the whole group. This can be implemented within your small group working.

Think-Pair-Share is usually referred to as a Kagan structure, but it was developed originally by Frank Lyman and Arlene Mindus in 1977 and adapted as part of the Kagan Structures.

Kagan Structures promote four major principles, following the acronym PIES:

- Positive Independence.
- Individual Accountability.
- Equal Participation.
- Simultaneous Interaction.

The above principles support pupil engagement and pupils taking responsibility for their own learning. There are some links in the further reading section of the chapter for you to explore Kagan strategies further.

There are many types of intervention programmes that may be happening in your schools. Here is an overview of some of the interventions that may be taking place.

- *Behaviour interventions*

A TA/LSA could carry out intervention work relating to specific strategies for a pupil to recognise when they are beginning to dysregulate, and when emotions are becoming unmanageable and therefore affecting their behaviour in the classroom. The TA/LSA should be trained in working with the pupil on strategies, and a support plan should be in place that gives clear guidance on the process and strategies to be used. It is important to remember that for the behaviour seen, there is an underlying issue or barrier that needs to be investigated or addressed too such as SEMH needs.

- *Classroom-based interventions*

Classroom-based interventions can be an effective strategy to support the development of pupils in a structured way without being removed from the class base. This can have positive effects on pupils as they are not seen as being singled out for additional support in the same way as when they are removed from the class. It also minimises disruption for the pupils as part of their day. However, distraction from other pupils and other teaching that may be happening at the same time will need to be considered. Pre-teaching could take place as a classroom-based intervention.

- *Collaborative interventions*

Group interventions will enable groups of pupils to rehearse subject content and knowledge through group discussions and teamwork. Pupils will be given the opportunity to listen to the contribution of other pupils, which can help them to generate or confirm their own ideas, or to challenge their thoughts and develop new thinking around a topic or area of discussion.

Group interventions will be delivering a specific programme based around gaps in curriculum knowledge and skills.

- *Social, emotional and well-being interventions*

Some interventions will not be based on academic progress, and will be centred around pupils' SEMH needs. These groups may include a grief or loss group, a nurture group, an exam anxiety group, or a communication skills group. These are just a few examples.

CASE STUDY

From Allaya an LSA.

Allaya worked as an LSA in a Year 5 class. She supported a range of pupils with additional needs, and was not fixed to working with a particular pupil on a one-to-one basis. Allaya often worked with groups of pupils, on specific skills or knowledge that had been identified. Sometimes her focus was supporting the class teacher through pre-teaching subject specific language prior to a lesson, at other times it would be working with a group relating to the lesson content.

Allaya was having difficulty when working with a particular group of pupils, with one pupil being quite challenging for her. When Zain was within the group, Allaya found that she spent a great deal of time managing disagreements rather than working with them on the things that she needed to.

Allaya met with the class teacher (Martha) during an assembly time to discuss the challenges she was having which was starting to cause her some concerns and anxiety around taking the group. Martha worked with Allaya to unpick what was happening, and suggested she observe the group dynamic while Allaya was taking them. This was in a supportive way and not a critical way, as the teacher knew that Zain could present with challenging behaviour if he became agitated or misunderstood the content of the lessons, and she empathised with Allaya. They decided to work on this collaboratively through discussion and planned a way forward.

Martha observed two group sessions from a distance while she was supporting and facilitating a task with other groups. She noticed that Zain was fine when he was working on his own, but when they were asked to discuss ideas within the group, arguments arose. Martha decided to explore this further with Zain and Allaya. They spoke with Zain to find out his perspective on how he felt when working within a group. Zain had a diagnosis of autism, and he would find turn taking in games difficult, he had on-going interventions to support and develop his skills in this; however, these didn't seem to be transferring over to his group work and discussions within the classroom. Zain said that he didn't always agree with other pupils' ideas, and some of them were silly and this annoyed him, and he preferred to do things on his own as they were his ideas which he liked. It was decided that to begin with, Allaya would enable Zain to write his discussion points on a whiteboard

(Continued)

by himself while the rest of the group discussed their ideas. This would give Zain the opportunity to explore his ideas within the time that he had. Martha also arranged for Allaya to join in with the intervention group that Zain was attending so that she could bring back some of the ideas, strategies and learning from the intervention, and apply them within her group work.

Allaya saw instant improvements for Zain and the group when he could work on his own, and she also began to develop her own skills and strategies to bring back to her group work from shadowing the interventions group. These included:

- setting up group rules to include being respectful of each other's ideas;
- taking time to facilitate each pupil to express their ideas, and not hurrying them;
- giving pupils roles within a task;
- modelling how to disagree politely and to give reasons why you disagree;
- using paired work within the group, rather than all pupils contributing to the whole group discussion.

Allaya was then able to apply these strategies across her teaching too.

- *One-to-one intervention*

This targeted support identifies specific areas of content knowledge and skills in which a pupil has gaps. These interventions provide the opportunity for a pupil to work directly and individually with a TA or LSA on very personalised targets, and there is greater scope of achievement and of accelerated learning via one-to-one interventions. These types of interventions are normally implemented in short bursts of approximately 20 minutes a session with several sessions a week.

The EEF (2021) outline that to implement this individual support in schools effectively, the following should happen:

- The accurate identification of the pupils who need the additional support. This could be done through the graduated approach, and pupils would be identified by the class teacher and the SENCo. This will be explored further in Chapter 8.
- The understanding of the learning gaps that each individual pupil has, and that the additional tuition is applied to address these gaps in curriculum knowledge and content.
- Ensure that the deliverer of the intervention is well prepared and having high-quality interactions with pupils such as giving well-planned feedback.
- Assessment from this should then be given to the class teacher on pupil progress and the tuition then needs adjusting accordingly to the needs of the pupil.
- One-to-one tuition should be well linked to the classroom content and must allow time for the teacher and the tutor to discuss the tuition, so that these links can

be made. This will ensure the knowledge and skills are being transferred from the tuition back into the classroom, and across curriculum content and subjects.
- The one-to-one tuition may be delivered by teachers, trained teaching assistants, academic mentors or tutors. Interventions are typically delivered over an extended period, often over several weeks or a term.

Ensure explicit connections are made between learning from everyday classroom and teaching and structured interventions.

When pupils are attending structured interventions, it is really important that this learning is then transferred across the curriculum. Making cognitive links are essential for application across the curriculum and strategies for the retrieval of knowledge and skills and then application need to be applied. Work with your TA/LSA to look at how these skills can be recalled and applied back in the classroom.

The EEF (2021) have an on-line toolkit for working with pupils on a one-to-one basis and implementing specific targeted interventions and tuition. Their research focus is based upon interventions that are being delivered to develop curriculum knowledge and skills.

Time for training and support for TAs/LSAs in school is short, some schools have very little availability for this (if any) and further needs to be done in this area to support schools with funding and training. A recommended text to pass on to your TA/LSA is *The Neurodiversity Handbook for Teaching Assistants and Learning Support Assistants; A guide for Learning Support Staff* (Alix, 2023b), which highlights supporting strategies from the perspective of a TA/LSA.

Working with Educational Professionals

Reflect

Name and list the educational professionals that you have either worked with, or heard of in school so far.

Are there any other professionals that you know of, and do you know what their roles are? As we work through the next section, make a note of any that you have not heard of before, and follow up with some additional reading of what that role looks like within your Local Authority (LA).

In education, we work with many different professionals to support SEND pupils. We work beyond delivering lessons in classes and become part of a multi-agency team to support pupils. Within each Local Authority (LA) some roles may look slightly different in the way that they are structured, or implemented, so it is important to find out what these roles look like within your own LA. Some may have slightly different names and titles too.

- Behaviour Support: this team will consist of advisors who will come into schools and support with strategies to implement as a teacher with your pupils. The team will also work closely with Behaviour Support Workers who work directly with parents and carers in the home, to join up the thinking around the strategies and support between the home and the school. Behaviour support advisors and behaviour support workers will collaborate closely together.
- Child and Adult Mental Health Service (CAMHS): the mental health team may support pupils for mental health concerns or anxiety. Pupils may be referred to CAMHS via the school SENCo, a GP, or parents. The pupil may attend group or individual sessions, which are normally over an allotted period of time, for example 6–8 sessions.
- Educational Psychologist (EP): the EP may assess a pupil in school, and within this assessment they might conduct tests and assessments to provide a report on the areas of difficulties for a pupil, and then provide a set of recommendations and supporting strategies and resources.
- Education Welfare Officer (EWO): an education welfare officer is responsible for monitoring pupil attendance at school. They may support SEND pupils, parents and schools when attendance is low. They may also attend multi-agency meetings to discuss pupil progress with attendance, and they can work with schools and LAs to issue penalties for absence if holiday is taken during term time.
- Medical Professionals: you may work with a range of medical professionals such as a GP, consultant or specialist nurse. It is likely that they may provide a support plan, guidance or attend multi-agency meetings around a specific medical care need.
- Specialist Teachers: these will be within a certain area, for example autism, neurological, or hearing or visual impairments such as the Qualified Teacher for the Visually Impaired (QTVI). They will visit the school and work directly with pupils on areas of need that have been included within their IEP or EHCP.
- Speech and Language Therapists: an outline of this role was given in Chapter 3.
- Social Worker: a pupil or family may be under the care or support of a social worker who will monitor the safeguarding of the pupil.
- Virtual Headteacher: this is a headteacher who oversees all of the Looked After Children (LAC)/ Children in Care (CiC) that are in care within their Local Authority (LA).

PROFESSIONAL DISCUSSION

Discuss with your mentor and SENCo whether you are able to shadow (or be an attendee) at a multi-agency meeting, so that you can begin to understand and see in practice how the services and professionals work together, to formulate support plans and provide services for SEND pupils.

Working with Parents and Carers

It can be a little daunting working with parents and carers as a trainee teacher. In a primary school, you will have quite a lot of contact with parents, and you will soon settle into this. You will have more contact in the earlier years, and less frequent contact as you enter Years 5 and 6 if pupils are able to take themselves to and from school, but regular contact with parents of your SEND pupils is important to maintain.

You may have contact during:

- school drop off and collection times;
- parents' evening or open days;
- SEND review meetings including one-plan or EHCP reviews;
- family open events such as the school fete and festival performances.

Some of these interactions will be more informal, and others formal.

It is important that you build relationships with parents and be open to listening to them. Often this can be at the start or the end of the day and it can be a quick catch up, passing over of information, or letting a parent know how their child is getting on. At other times there will be more formal reviews of progress made towards targets and plans for the next steps of support.

Sometimes parents can become frustrated by the lack of progress made by their child, or feel that the support that is in place isn't enough for them. Often it can be a misunderstanding regarding expectations in the classroom, and if difficult conversations are needed with parents regarding your SEND pupils, then you need to seek support and guidance from your SENCo who can support you in explaining how provision is allocated. Parents may also have their own barriers to education and to engaging with schools, such as having their own poor literacy skills, or fears due to their own negative experiences of school.

There are many positive things that you can do to develop your relationships with your SEND pupils' parents including:

- consider parents as partners in your pupils' education and progress;
- ensure that you allocate time to share positive information about your pupil with them regularly;
- make time to listen to their concerns;
- develop a relationship that has mutual respect;
- smile and use open body language;
- find out more about their child, ask questions about their routines, and what works well for them at home;
- invite parents in to join the class for parts of the end of the lesson to understand what the classroom looks like for their child;
- arrange for parents to meet with other SEND parents through school coffee mornings that may be in place;

- do not contradict a diagnosis; pupils may show things differently at school and home and parents may see different behaviour. You are not qualified to diagnose;
- use appropriate language and terminology about SEND, never joke about a child's needs.

Parents may need support with:

- preparing to talk or give information at a more formal meeting or review;
- understanding terminology relating to education and SEND;
- expressing themselves or with language if English is not their first language;
- sharing their own perspectives and thoughts.

They may need:

- time to prepare for meetings;
- a friend or family member to accompany them;
- accessible information in a format that is suitable for them;
- professionals to avoid jargon or explain terms that are used.

As part of your teacher training course, you will begin to develop your relationships with the parents of the pupils in your class. The more you have contact time with them, and get to know their child, the more confident you will be in discussing their progress, and any challenges with them. You will shadow parents' evenings in terms one and two and you may lead on some pupils' parents' evening discussion as you move to term three of your training.

Activity

Discuss with your mentor to attend and shadow any review meetings that you can.

You may also be asked for your input during these as you move into your final teaching block and take responsibility for pupil learning and progress.

Chapter Summary

This chapter has looked in detail at working with TAs and LSAs to support your SEND pupils. The section has given you strategies on how to support your TA/LSA in working with your SEND pupils. It has considered the EEF (2018) recommendations on good practice and use of TAs/LSAs and discussed areas of these to focus on when supporting TA/LSA practice.

The case study examined how a teacher supported their LSA to work with a challenging group of pupils, and you can reflect upon your developing role and the teachers' standard relating to working with support staff.

The next section gave an overview of working with other educational professionals. This will be an important element of working with SEND pupils, and you will need to develop your experience here as you move through your Early Career Teacher (ECT) years and take full responsibility for your class and SEND pupils.

The final section looked at working with parents and carers with a focus on developing positive and open relationships with them.

Glossary of Key Terms

- Teaching Assistant (TA) – A member of support staff that will work across the whole class offering academic support to all pupils and being a good role model to them. They are directed by the class teacher to work with different groups depending on the focus.
- Learning Support Assistant (LSA) – A member of support staff that will often work one-to-one with pupils, they may also have a pastoral role, and they may support or lead on the implementation and conducting of specific interventions.

Further Reading

- Alix, S. (2023a). *The Neurodiversity Handbook for Trainee Teachers*. London: Sage.
- Alix, S. (2023b). *The Neurodiversity Handbook for Teaching Assistants and Learning Support Assistants; A Guide for Learning Support Staff, SENCOs and Students*. London: Routledge Publications.
- Department for Education (2014). Professional Standards for Teaching Assistants. https://neu.org.uk/advice/professional-standards-teaching-assistants
- Education Endowment Foundation (2018). Making Best Use of Teaching Assistants. https://educationendowmentfoundation.org.uk/education-evidence/guidance-reports/teaching-assistants?utm_source=/education-evidence/guidance-reports/teaching-assistants&utm_medium=search&utm_campaign=site_searchh&search_term
- Education Endowment Foundation (2018). Working with Parents to Support Children's Learning. https://educationendowmentfoundation.org.uk/education-evidence/guidance-reports/supporting-parents
- Education Endowment Foundation (2021). One to One Tuition. https://educationendowmentfoundation.org.uk/education-evidence/teaching-learning-toolkit/one-to-one-tuition
- Iris Connect, How I support SEND Pupils. https://blog.irisconnect.com/uk/send-teaching
- Kagan cooperative learning structures. https://education.wm.edu/centers/sli/events/ESL%20101/kagan-cl-structures.pdf
- Kagan, it's all about engagement. https://www.kaganonline.com/free_articles/dr_spencer_kagan/264/The-quot-E-quot-of-PIES

Links to the Teachers' Standards

- *5. Adapt teaching to respond to the strengths and needs of all pupils*; have a secure understanding of how a range of factors can inhibit pupils' ability to learn, and how best to overcome these; have a clear understanding of the needs of all pupils, including those with special educational needs; those of high ability; those with English as an additional language; those with disabilities; and be able to use and evaluate distinctive teaching approaches to engage and support them.
- *8. Fulfil wider professional responsibilities*; make a positive contribution to the wider life and ethos of the school; develop effective professional relationships with colleagues, knowing how and when to draw on advice and specialist support; deploy support staff effectively; take responsibility for improving teaching through appropriate professional development, responding to advice and feedback from colleagues; communicate effectively with parents with regard to pupils' achievements and well-being.

References

Alix, S. (2023a). *The Neurodiversity Handbook for Trainee Teachers*. London: Sage.

Alix, S. (2023b). *The Neurodiversity Handbook for Teaching Assistants and Learning Support Assistants; A Guide for Learning Support Staff, SENCOs and Students*. London: Routledge Publications.

Education Endowment Foundation (2018). Making Best Use of Teaching Assistants. https://educationendowmentfoundation.org.uk/education-evidence/guidance-reports/teaching-assistants?utm_source=/education-evidence/guidance-reports/teaching-assistants&utm_medium=search&utm_campaign=site_searchh&search_term

Webster, R., Blatchford, P. and Russell, A., (2013). Challenging and changing how schools use teaching assistants: Findings from the Effective Deployment of Teaching Assistants project. *School Leadership and Management*, 33 (1).

8

Assessing Pupil Needs through the Graduated Approach

Chapter Aims

- To provide an overview of the types of assessment in schools and their purpose.
- To gain an understanding of current SEND practice including High Quality Teaching for all, Ordinarily Available provision for all, and targeted support.
- To gain an understanding of adaptive teaching in the classroom.
- To gain an understanding of the graduated approach, and the teacher's responsibility in this process.

Links to the Core Content Framework (CCF)

How Pupils Learn

- ***Learn that*** prior knowledge plays an important role in how pupils learn; committing some key facts to their long-term memory is likely to help pupils learn more complex ideas.

Adaptive Teaching

- ***Learn that*** seeking to understand pupils' differences, including their different levels of prior knowledge and potential barriers to learning, is an essential part of teaching.
- ***Learn that*** pupils are likely to learn at different rates and to require different levels and types of support from teachers to succeed.
- ***Learn how to*** receive clear, consistent and effective mentoring in supporting pupils with a range of additional needs, including how to use the SEND Code of Practice, which provides additional guidance on supporting pupils with SEND effectively.
- ***Learn how to*** identify pupils who need new content further broken down.
- ***Learn how to*** make use of formative assessment.

Assessment

- ***Learn that*** effective assessment is critical to teaching because it provides teachers with information about pupils' understanding and needs.
- ***Learn that*** before using any assessment, teachers should be clear about the decision it will be used to support and be able to justify its use.
- ***Learn that*** working with colleagues to identify efficient approaches to assessment is important; assessment can become onerous and have a disproportionate impact on workload.
- ***Learn how to*** discuss and analyse with expert colleagues how to plan formative assessment tasks linked to lesson objectives and think ahead about what would indicate understanding (e.g. by using hinge questions to pinpoint knowledge gaps).
- ***Learn how to*** discuss and analyse with expert colleagues how to choose, where possible, externally validated materials, used in controlled conditions when required to make summative assessments.
- ***Learn how to*** draw conclusions about what pupils have learned by looking at patterns of performance over a number of assessments with support and scaffolding from expert colleagues (e.g. appreciating that assessments draw inferences about learning from performance).

Introduction

This chapter will be looking at assessing pupils' SEN through the use of the graduated approach. To begin to understand the graduated approach, first, knowledge of the elements that underpin classroom practice such as High Quality Teaching and Adaptive

Teaching are needed. These core pedagogies contribute to the teaching within the graduated approach cycle.

There have been recent shifts and changes in terminology around assessment and provision for pupils, and there is a mix of terminology being used in schools. As part of this chapter, we will look at these terms, what they mean, what they look like in the classroom, and how they relate to the graduated approach. These approaches are underpinned by the evidence base from the Education Endowment Foundation (EEF).

I discuss the graduated approach with a focus around neurodiversity in *The Neurodiversity Handbook for Trainee Teachers* (Alix, 2023). This chapter will take a different focus around the terms and implementation of teaching approaches linked to the graduated approach. Both complement each other when thinking about your SEND/ Neurodivergent pupils.

The Types and Purpose of Assessment in School

You will have no doubt been using both formative and summative assessment in your host class by now. Below is a short summary of each.

Formative Assessment

Formative assessment happens on a daily basis and it forms part of reviewing what you plan and teach your pupils. Formative assessment will include asking open and closed questions, quizzes, polls, self-assessment and peer-assessment. This type of assessment is part of live monitoring, and feeds in to your following planning so that you can support pupil progress on a daily and lesson-by-lesson basis.

Summative Assessment

Summative assessment happens at the end of a period or block of teaching, such as at the end of a half term or term, or the end of a particular topic or unit of work. Formal summative assessment results in examinations such as Standardised Assessment Tests (SATs) that you will experience in primary schools, or General Certificate of Secondary Education (GCSEs) at the end of pupils' secondary education.

Reflect

At this stage of your training:

- What forms of formative and summative assessment are you becoming more confident with implementing?

- Where is your experience and evidence of this development?
- Are there any areas of assessment relating to the CCF that you still need further practical experience of?

Current Terminology, Meanings and Implications in the classroom; Quality First Teaching (QFT) and High Quality Teaching (HQT).

Quality First Teaching (QFT) and High Quality Teaching (HQT) are terms used for the good quality of teaching that should be happening in a classroom on a daily basis. This teaching should have high expectations for all learners and be available for all learners. This is also really important for your SEND pupils. Teaching and assessment are intrinsically linked; your assessment of pupils is running through everything that you teach, and at each stage of planning, delivery, and review of each lesson.

This is why it is important to look at these elements now, before we move on to the graduated approach.

What is Quality First Teaching?

Quality First Teaching has been a popular term, used for several years within the education sector and by teaching staff. It evolved from the Department for Children, Schools and Families policy document called *Personalised Learning; a Practical Guide* (2008). It outlined the importance of higher levels of support for all pupils to succeed in their education achievements.

The DfE Code of Practice (2015) states:

> High quality teaching that is differentiated and personalised will meet the individual needs of the majority of children and young people. Some children and young people need educational provision that is additional to or different from this. This is special educational provision under Section 21 of the Children and Families Act 2014. Schools and colleges must use their best endeavours to ensure that such provision is made for those who need it. Special educational provision is underpinned by high quality teaching and is compromised by anything less.

As you can see, the above quote from the DfE (2015) talks about 'High Quality Teaching' and yet the term 'Quality First Teaching' was coined and used, with only recently a clearer use of the term High Quality Teaching, which we will discuss in the next section.

The essential characteristics of Quality First Teaching are:

1 Using clearly designed lesson plans.
2 Giving plenty of opportunities to involve and engage with pupils.

3 Using appropriate modelling, explaining, and questioning for pupils to engage with higher levels of critical thinking skills.
4 Providing pupils with the chance to talk both individually and in groups.
5 Having an expectation that pupils will accept responsibility for their own learning and work independently.
6 Regularly using encouragement and praise to engage and motivate pupils.

So, what is High Quality Teaching?

Terminology is changing, and there is a shift from using Quality First Teaching to using High Quality Teaching (HQT), which is the term used within the Code of Practice (2015) as seen above.

One of the approaches that is specific to HQT is the five-a-day approach (EEF, 2021) which has been outlined further in Chapter 4. As a reminder, the key areas of the five-a-day approach are:

1 Explicit instruction – Teacher-led approaches with a focus on clear explanations, modelling, and frequent checks for understanding. This is then followed by guided practice before independent practice.
2 Cognitive and metacognitive strategies – Managing cognitive load is crucial if new content is to be transferred into students' long-term memory. Provide opportunities for students to plan, monitor and evaluate their own learning.
3 Scaffolding – When students are working on a written task, provide a supportive tool or resource such as a writing frame, or a partially completed example. Aim to provide less support of this nature throughout the course of the lesson, week, or term.
4 Flexible grouping – Allocate groups temporarily, based on their current level of mastery. This could, for example, be a group that comes together to get some additional spelling instruction based on current need, before re-joining the main class.
5 Using technology – Technology can be used by a teacher to model worked examples; it can be used by a student to help them to learn, to practise and to record their learning. For instance, you might use a class visualiser to share students' work or to jointly rework an incorrect model.

Education Endowment Foundation (EEF) (2021)

Both QFT and HQT are the base layer of tiered approaches to support all pupils and to support your SEND pupils. Figure 8.1 shows these models side by side to demonstrate a comparison.

The terms are used interchangeably, and there is some discussion as to whether they are the same thing or not. Different models will show a different interpretation of what

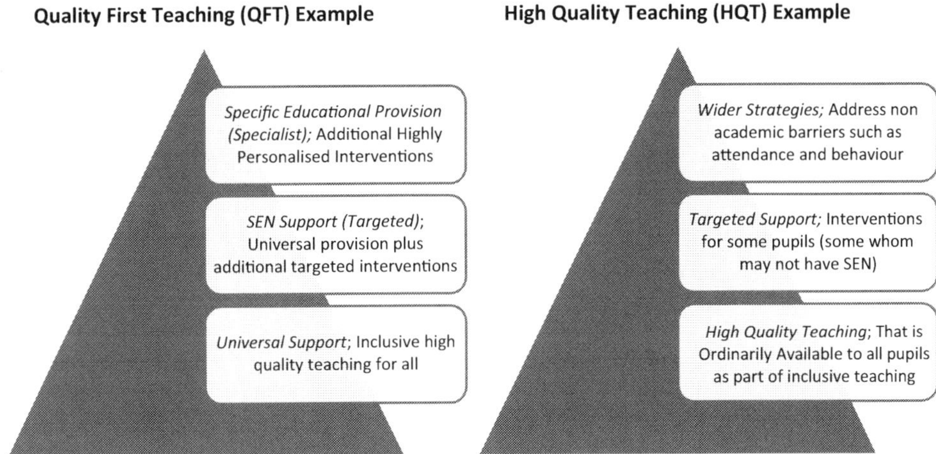

Figure 8.1 Models demonstrating examples of Quality First Teaching and High Quality Teaching.

is meant by the approaches, but generally there is a consensus that there is a base layer of universal teaching for all through QFT/HQT and adaptive teaching as part of this level, with targeted support and interventions as the next layer up, and then with a top tier of further additionality in some form. High Quality Teaching has become the preferred term for the base layer, supported by the evidence base from the EEF (2021). I have tried to demonstrate a distinction, but as terminology evolves, so does the understanding underpinning this.

Targeted academic support

As you will see, both models contain a mid-level of targeted academic support which is a level above provision such as QFT/HQT for all pupils. Most pupils will benefit from the focus on high-quality, whole-class teaching. However, some children may require extra, targeted support that is tailored to their specific needs and to support them to get their learning back on track when they have a gap in their knowledge or have fallen behind in a particular area.

Additional interventions could include revisiting foundational knowledge, practising core skills, or pre-learning upcoming content for lessons. Interventions need to complement and link to the curriculum being covered within the class.

The TARGET model draws from a range of EEF interventions and programmes, and outlines a summary of evidence-based targeted interventions that are proven to be successful:

- **T**iming
- **A**ssessment
- **R**esourcing

- **G**ive it time
- **E**xpert delivery
- **T**eacher links

Intervention sessions should be regular, for example two to five times a week, and they should be brief, only lasting between fifteen minutes to an hour. They should last for between eight and twenty weeks. The research shows that these interventions should be delivered by a qualified teacher, or a highly skilled and trained teaching assistant. If it is the teaching assistant delivering the interventions, then, as we saw in Chapter 7, there should be good communication between the teaching assistant and the classroom teacher on the progress of pupils, and they should be ensuring that contextual links are made back in the classroom, with the learning that has taken place during the intervention.

PROFESSIONAL **DISCUSSION**

Jot down a list of targeted interventions that you know are taking place for some of your pupils in your class.

- What are they?
- What are they for?

Discuss with your mentor how they receive feedback on the progress your pupils are making within these intervention groups.

- How do they know?
- What do they do with that information?
- How do they feed this back into the learning within the whole class?

Wider strategies

'Wider strategies' form the top layer of the pyramid in Figure 8.1. This layer includes strategies to improve positive learning behaviours and support to move pupils back on track when there is a non-academic barrier such as poor attendance (EEF, 2022).

Activity

Focus on 'High Quality Teaching, Targeted Support and Wider Strategies'. Observe a lesson by your mentor, or another experienced teacher, and note down the elements of High Quality Teaching that you can observe in practice.

- How do these elements make up the lesson?

Discuss with the class teacher after the observation.

- How did they decide to implement each of these elements?
- What did they decide to implement before the lesson as part of their planning?
- What did they change and implement during the lesson as part of a flexible approach?

Adaptive Teaching

Adaptive teaching forms part of High Quality Teaching, and it is a central element and core standard within the Core Content Framework (CCF), which is your training entitlement, and the Early Career Framework (ECF). There has been a shift from using the term, and the practice of 'differentiation' in schools. The term is still held within documentation such as the Teachers' Standards, and it can be argued that it has its place as an element of adaptive teaching. Differentiation could be seen as a normal part of everyday practice within classrooms just a few years and months ago, and I am sure that on your teacher training journey that some of you may come across this being the sole method of support happening in some classes, in some schools. Differentiation would be using different handouts for pupils – they may contain a different level of work, or even a different topic or lesson aims if it was deemed that the level of original work was inaccessible by a pupil. The effect of using this as a sole support strategy for pupils was that a ceiling of achievement or attainment was being lowered on to them. They did not have the opportunity to be supported, or to progress with, the learning that other pupils were working on or achieving in their classes.

Adaptive teaching sets the same targets, goals and objectives for all pupils, aiming for the top, and then provides different levels of scaffolded support to pupils who need this. This should be part of High Quality Teaching and what is ordinarily available to all pupils. The scaffolding then targets pupil starting points to support their progress. These scaffolds are taken away as the pupil becomes more proficient in the concept, process or knowledge being taught.

So, how can you do this?

- *Provide scaffolded support so that all learners have the opportunity to meet expectations* – support all pupils to work towards the same goal but break the learning down.
- *Balance the input of new content to retrieved content so that learners master important concepts* – give the right amount of time to pupils' mastery.
- *Know your learners and provide targeted support* – make use of well-designed resources and planning to connect new content with pupils' prior knowledge or provide additional pre-teaching if learners lack critical knowledge.
- *Use Assessment for Learning in the classroom – in essence check, reflect and respond* – create assessments that are fit for purpose, moving away from the sole use of end of unit assessments.
- *Make effective use of your teaching assistants* – deliver high quality one-to-one and small group support using structured interventions.

(Raso, 2023)

The Engagement Model

Previously in schools, P-levels or P-scales were used to assess pupils working below the National Curriculum levels or Age-Related Expectations (ARE). The engagement model has replaced these scales and has been designed to support pupils not working at Age Related Expectations (ARE).

The model uses a pupil-centred approach and it focuses on the abilities and achievements of a pupil rather than any disabilities and deficits. This model is used alongside the graduated approach which is outlined in the next section.

The model examines and monitors progress across the four broad areas of need within the Code of Practice:

- Communication and interaction
- Cognition and learning
- Social, emotional, and mental health
- Sensory and/or physical needs

This model assesses not only progress in each area, but also pupil engagement in developing new skills and the pupil's progress against outcomes and targets within their EHCPs (Watts, 2022). The engagement model is mainly seen being implemented in schools with specialist provision but speak with your class teacher or SENCo and ask if it is implemented within your school for any pupils. Links to further reading on the engagement model can be found at the end of this chapter.

The Graduated Approach

The Special Educational Needs Register (SEN Register)

Pupils who need additional support and are making less than expected progress are added to the SEN register. This is a register that each school holds to keep track of pupils requiring additional support. Pupils may be added to the register, or if they are making good progress and no longer need to be on the register, they can be removed. Adding and removing to and from the register can happen at any time.

When pupils are added to the register, the SENCo will have identified their main area of need, and this will be listed as per the four broad areas of need that we have seen in Part II of the book. For pupils on the register, the assess-plan-do-review cycle as per the graduated approach will be followed, as outlined in the following section.

The Graduated Approach

The graduated approach is used as a form of overarching assessment and gathering of information, to inform what is needed for a pupil when they need a different sort of approach to the majority of pupils in the class. It may be that they are moving from the bottom tier of support within the models in Figure 8.1, which includes a level of universal support including high quality teaching and what is ordinarily available to your pupils, to a targeted level of support in which specific interventions may need to be included.

The graduated approach is comprised of a four-part cycle: *assess, plan, do, review*. The cycle is worked through by yourself as the class teacher, in collaboration with the SENCo and with support and input from parents and carers, and the pupil themselves. The cycle ensures that by exploring the needs and challenges that the pupil faces, the right support for them can be identified, implemented, and then reviewed and amended.

It is important to note, that at the centre of this approach is the pupil and their family, and gathering their views is vital in contributing, informing, and beginning this cycle.

In the past, the SENCo held responsibility for the management of all of the pupils with additional needs; however, this has changed with the newest Code of Practice. The responsibility is now shared, and every member of school staff has an important role to play and responsibility to hold in the development, support and progress of each pupil. The class teacher has more responsibility now and has the overview of each of their pupils with SEND within their class. They lead on the graduated approach for their pupils, and the review of any support plans that are in place for them. As a trainee teacher, it is important for you to understand this cycle and process and begin to take on the responsibility for your pupils during this process as you progress through your teacher training year and towards your final block practice.

Let's outline the stages within the graduated approach (some of this is outlined and linked to the Neurodiversity model by Alix (2023)):

Stage 1 – Assess

This initial stage includes gathering information from the daily types of formative assessment so that an overview of where the pupil is at can be formed. As the class teacher, your role is central to gathering this information, and you will be responsible for this area. It will include identification of any barriers that might be in the way of the pupil making progress that is in line with their peers.

You will have a discussion with the pupil and their parents or carers (either on your own, or with the SENCo) to establish their views on any challenges that your pupil may have. You will be looking for any gaps in knowledge, understanding or skills for the pupil, and whether any further assessments that the school can provide might be beneficial at this stage. The SENCo will also consider whether any referrals to other agencies or exploration of further external assessments might be useful.

Internal school assessments and tests might include: reading, spelling and maths tests; profiling tools for the assessment of speech and language challenges; communication assessments that may include looking at body language and responses to scenarios and behaviours; diagnostic assessments linked to Cognitive Abilities Tests (CATs) and the use of screening tools for the possibility of dyslexia or dyspraxia.

Your SENCo will arrange for any of these additional assessments to take place, and there may be a waiting list within your school for this, depending on who is conducting the assessments, their expertise, other pupils waiting to be assessed, and the workload of the person undertaking the assessment. Often these types of assessment are carried out by the SENCo themselves, or a specialist member of the support staff team who has had further training in the area and the implementation of the tool or test.

There may be restrictions on some types of assessment; for example, some dyslexia screening tools can only be used with pupils over the age of seven or eight years old.

Stage 2 – Plan

At this stage, the information that was gathered in stage 1 is discussed and a plan formulated that will include support for the pupil based upon their emerging needs. The planning process will include everyone that is part of the support network for the pupil including the pupil themselves, parents or carers, the class teacher, and the SENCo. If there are any external agencies involved in supporting the pupil, they will be included too.

Included within the plan, targets are set that are tightly focused around specific areas that have been identified. Each target should have action steps that will be granular and support the work towards the target. It will identify what the support is, who will implement this support, who will review it, and how and when it will take place. It will also include specific teaching strategies and any resources linked to this.

The plan will have a timeline with review dates set. The plan needs to be shared with everyone involved in working with the pupil, and this will include you as part of that team. If you are not included in a circulation list, ensure that you sit with your class teacher to read the plan together and to understand your role in working on the targets for any pupils you are working with. The plan may be presented as an IEP, one plan, one-page profile, pupil passport or individual provision map.

Stage 3 – Do

The responsibility of implementing the plan at this 'do' stage is held with you, the class teacher. The implementation should be carried out on a daily basis and provision being implemented at all times. It could include strategies such as:

- High Quality Teaching, including the five-a-day approach (as outlined earlier in the chapter);
- implementing specific individual strategies or interventions which might include 1:1 or group support in maths, English, communication, or social skills;
- directing staff to implement support or strategies such as working with the TA or LSA;
- using formative assessment to monitor and review progress;
- adjusting strategies in relation to progress made;
- communicating with the SENCo, parents and carers with the progress being made.

Stage 4 - Review

The review stage is the final stage before the process is then repeated and the cycle begins again. A meeting is held in which the targets are discussed and evaluated; where has progress been made? Have any further barriers been identified? It is an opportunity to reflect upon what is currently in place and what progress has been made.

These meetings are normally held separately and may be carried out by the SENCo, the class teacher, or a combination of them.

In preparation for the review stage, you, as the class teacher, will gather evidence towards the targets to be used within the review. This might include considering your thoughts and evidence on:

- Has the pupil achieved the targets set? Have you got any evidence to support this?
- If a pupil has not met a target, what progress has been made towards the target?
- Which interventions have been successful?
- What changes might need to be made?

At this point, it is decided whether the pupil has made enough progress to be taken off this graduated approach, or enters another cycle of assess, plan, review, do.

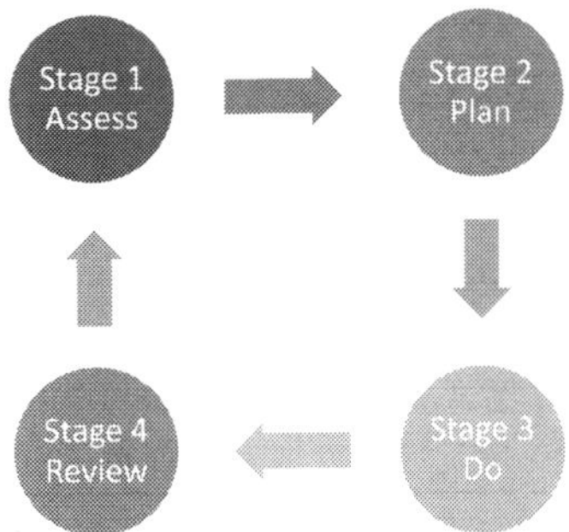

Figure 8.2 An overview model of the graduated approach as outlined in NASEN (2022).

The following questions will need to be considered at each stage of the graduated approach cycle and you can consider these when working with your pupils:
Stage 1 – Assess

- Is the pupil able to access the curriculum?
- Is the learning environment appropriately set up? What else could you do?
- What are the pupil's interests and strengths? How are these included?

Stage 2 – Plan

- Share any concerns with your class teacher
- What are your pupil's views?
- How have you built on the strengths of the pupil?

Stage 3 – Do

- What has been achieved?
- What has worked well? What hasn't?

Stage 4 – Review

- What else might be useful or needed?

NASEN (2022)

CASE STUDY

From an Early Career Teacher, Aviv.

Aviv had recently taken on his first class in a large three-form entry primary school, he was teaching Year 4.

At the end of his teacher training year, Aviv was able to spend the last two weeks of the year in his new class getting to know the pupils and the school policies and procedures. He had spoken with the SENCo regarding the IEPs for two of his pupils and had spent some time over the summer familiarising himself with their targets, considering what he might need to do to support them in class through High Quality Teaching and adaptive teaching. However, when Aviv started in September, he had an additional new pupil join his class, Frieda. He had been unaware that Frieda would be joining him until the first day of term as she was new to the area.

As the first few weeks progressed, Aviv became familiar with teaching his new class, the school ethos and general management of the school, and implementing his classroom strategies. Over the first half term he began to gain a much better understanding of his pupils, where they were at in terms of their learning, and the progress that they were making. Towards the end of this first half term, Aviv began to have some concerns regarding Frieda's progress. At first, he wasn't sure whether the lack of progress was due to the school and home move, or whether Frieda had unidentified and unmet needs.

When half term arrived, Aviv was feeling a little exhausted (as to be expected at the end of the first few weeks as an ECT!) and enjoyed stepping back from the classroom for a few days, but Frieda was on his mind as he was unsure what to do next.

Activity

Consider the case study of Aviv and Frieda above. Imagine this is you at the start of your first year as an ECT, you may be juggling a new class and school, and getting to know your pupils.

- What advice would you give Aviv?
- Who should he speak to about Frieda?

- What would be the next steps?
- What is likely to happen next to move forward to support Frieda?

Draw up a plan of actions to take, and possible next steps.

For further information on the Assessment Tool types used in schools, External Assessments to support the graduated approach and Access Arrangements for pupil exams, these are outlined in The Neurodiversity Handbook for Trainee Teachers *(Alix, 2023).*

Chapter Summary

This chapter has looked at the core teaching approaches and the graduated approach to assessment. It started with a recap of formative and summative assessment, followed by a detailed discussion and analysis of Quality First Teaching and High Quality Teaching, with a comparative model. The High Quality Teaching model also considered the layers of targeted support and wider strategies. The chapter then covered the move from differentiation to a broader inclusive approach of adaptive teaching. There was then a brief overview of the engagement model which is commonly used in special schools.

The final section of the chapter focused on the graduated approach, and the teacher's role within this approach. You then provided Aviv with some advice on his next steps with Frieda as he settled into his first ECT year.

Glossary of Key Terms

- Adaptive Teaching – Scaffolded support for pupils to achieve the same aims, goals and objectives as all pupils.
- Engagement model – The engagement model has replaced P-scales as a form of assessment mainly used within special schools and has been designed to support pupils not working at Age Related Expectations (ARE).
- Formative assessment – Formative assessment happens on a daily basis and it forms part of you reviewing what you plan and teach your pupils.
- High Quality Teaching – The current term used in schools to represent high quality teaching available to all pupils, and that is ordinarily available.
- Quality First Teaching – Quality First Teaching has been a popular term that has been used for several years within the education sector and by teaching staff. High quality teaching that is differentiated and personalised.
- Summative assessment – Summative assessment is a formal assessment of a block of work which happens at the end of a period or block of teaching, such as at the end of a half term or term, or a particular topic or unit of work.

Further Reading

- Education Endowment Foundation (EEF) (2021). High Quality Teaching Benefits Pupils with SEND; The five-a-day principle. https://d2tic4wvo1iusb.cloudfront.net/production/eef-guidance-reports/send/Five-a-day-poster_1.1.pdf?v=1690638622
- Education Endowment Foundation (EEF) (2022). High Quality Teaching. https://educationendowmentfoundation.org.uk/support-for-schools/school-planning-support/1-high-quality-teaching
- Education Endowment Foundation (EEF) (2022). Moving Forwards, Making a Difference. A Planning Guide for Schools 2022–23. https://d2tic4wvo1iusb.cloudfront.net/production/documents/School_Planning_Guide_2022-23.pdf?v=1691221565
- National Association for Special Educational Needs (NASEN) (2022). Teacher Handbook: SEND; Embedding Inclusive Practice. Education Endowment Foundation (EEF). https://www.wholeschoolsend.org.uk/resources/teacher-handbook-send
- Watts, C. (2022). How to Use the Engagement Model in Schools. https://www.highspeedtraining.co.uk/hub/the-engagement-model-in-schools/

Links to the Teachers' Standards

- *2. Promote good progress and outcomes by pupils;* be accountable for pupils' attainment, progress and outcomes; be aware of pupils' capabilities and their prior knowledge, and plan teaching to build on these; guide pupils to reflect on the progress they have made and their emerging needs
- *6. Make accurate and productive use of assessment:* know and understand how to assess the relevant subject and curriculum areas, including statutory assessment requirements; make use of formative and summative assessment to secure pupils' progress; use relevant data to monitor progress, set targets, and plan subsequent lessons

References

Alix, S. (2023). *The Neurodiversity Handbook for Trainee Teachers*. London: Sage.

Department for Children, Schools and Families (DfCSF) (2008). Personalised Learning; a Practical Guide. https://dera.ioe.ac.uk/id/eprint/8447/7/00844-2008DOM-EN_Redacted.pdf

Department for Education (DfE) (2015). Special Educational Needs and Disabilities Code of Practice; 0 to 25 Years. DfE.

Education Endowment Foundation (EEF) (2021). High Quality Teaching Benefits Pupils with SEND; The five-a-day principle. https://d2tic4wvo1iusb.cloudfront.net/production/eef-guidance-reports/send/Five-a-day-poster_1.1.pdf?v=1690638622

Education Endowment Foundation (EEF) (2022). High Quality Teaching. https://educationendowmentfoundation.org.uk/support-for-schools/school-planning-support/1-high-quality-teaching

Education Endowment Foundation (EEF) (2022). Moving Forwards, Making a Difference. A Planning Guide for Schools 2022–23. https://d2tic4wvo1iusb.cloudfront.net/production/documents/School_Planning_Guide_2022-23.pdf?v=1691221565

National Association for Special Educational Needs (NASEN) (2022). Teacher Handbook: SEND; Embedding Inclusive Practice. Education Endowment Foundation (EEF). https://www.wholeschoolsend.org.uk/resources/teacher-handbook-send

Raso, G. (2023). From Differentiation to Adaptive Teaching; What Does this Really Mean? NACE. https://www.nace.co.uk/blogpost/1761881/486112/From-differentiation-to-adaptive-teaching--what-does-this-really-mean#:~:text=Adaptive%20teaching%20is%20a%20focus,providing%20different%20levels%20of%20support.

UK Government (2010). The Equality Act 2010. https://www.legislation.gov.uk/ukpga/2010/15/contents

Watts, C. (2022) How to Use the Engagement Model in Schools. https://www.highspeedtraining.co.uk/hub/the-engagement-model-in-schools/

9

Education, Health and Care Plans (EHCP/EHC plans)

Chapter Aims

- To know what an Education, Health and Care Plan (EHCP/EHC plan) is.
- To know what an Education and Health Care Needs Assessment (EHCNA/EHC needs assessment) is.
- To understand the role of the Local Authority (LA) in carrying out an EHCNA.
- To understand the role of the LA in issuing an EHC plan, and then reviewing it.
- To understand the role of the SENCo in applying for an EHC needs assessment.
- To understand the role of the class teacher in applying for an EHC needs assessment.
- To understand the role of the SENCo in implementing the EHC plan and reviewing it.
- To understand the role of the teacher in implementing the EHC plan and then reviewing it.

Links to the Core Content Framework (CCF)

Adaptive Teaching

- ***Learn that*** pupils with special educational needs or disabilities are likely to require additional or adapted support; working closely with colleagues, families and pupils to understand barriers and identify effective strategies is essential.

Professional Behaviours

- ***Learn that*** building effective relationships with parents, carers and families can improve pupils' motivation, behaviour and academic success.

Introduction

This chapter has a very specific focus: to look in detail at Education, Health and Care plans, starting with exploring what an EHC plan is, who it is for, and who can apply for one. The chapter will then look at the assessment process to gain an EHC plan and the role of the SENCo and the teacher within this process. There will be an overview of the position of the Local Authority (LA) and their legal position in carrying out the assessment, and then issuing a plan. The final parts of the chapter will explore the detail of the implementation and review of the plan, what this looks like in the classroom, and what the class teacher will be doing as part of their legal duties to uphold the plan.

There are five stages to an Education and Health Care (EHC) plan:

- Identifying needs of children with SEND.
- Conducting an EHC needs assessment.
- Creating an Education, Health and Care plan.
- Implementing the final EHC plan.
- Regularly reviewing the EHC plan.

Many documents relating to EHC plans will refer to the 'child or young person'; I will refer to the 'pupil' throughout as I will be taking a school perspective so that you can relate this to your own experience as a developing teacher.

Reflection

Jot down some thoughts around the following:

- What do you know about EHC plans?
- Do you have any pupils in your teacher training class that have an EHC plan?

- If so, have you seen their EHC plan, or the outcomes that they are working towards?
- Can you identify the provision that is in their plan happening in practice?
- What does this look like?

What is an Education, Health and Care Plan?

An Education, Health and Care (EHC) plan is a legal document for children and young people aged up to the age of 25 years who need more support than is available through special educational needs support as outlined in Figure 8.1 in the previous chapter.

An EHC plan identifies educational, health and social needs, and sets out the additional support to meet those needs within the plan, and the outcomes that pupils would like to achieve. It can also give further options for a school setting for pupils to attend, such as a special school.

The Local Authority (LA) to the child, carries out the assessment once an application has been submitted and agreed to proceed to the assessment. A request for an assessment can be made by a young person themselves if they are aged 16 to 25 years, or by anyone who thinks that the child or young person need one, such as a teacher, a doctor, a health visitor, parents and family. If the LA proceed to an assessment, once this assessment is in process, then they will tell you within 16 weeks whether an EHC plan is going to be made for your child/pupil.

In summary, the purpose of an EHC plan is to:

- record the views, interests and aspirations of the parents and pupil;
- provide a full description of the pupil's special educational needs and any health and social care needs;
- establish outcomes across education, health and social care based on the pupil's needs and aspirations;
- specify the provision required and how education, health and care services will work together to meet the pupil's needs, and support the achievement of the agreed outcomes;
- enable the parents to request a particular school or college.

What Does an EHC Plan Look Like?

There is no standard format for the plan, so there will be slight differences from LA to LA. However, every plan must have particular sections that are labelled in the following way so that all areas are covered, and the provision needed is set out clearly.

The sections needed are:

- A: The views, interests and aspirations of you and your child.
- B: Special Educational Needs (SEN).
- C: Health needs related to SEN.

- D: Social care needs related to SEN.
- E: Outcomes – how the extra help will benefit the child.
- F: Special educational provision (support).
- G: Health provision.
- H: Social care provision.
- I: Placement – type and name of school or other institution.
- J: Personal budget arrangements.
- K: Advice and information – a list of the information gathered during the EHC needs assessment.

As you will see, some of the sections correspond: the needs are outlined in section B, and the provision is outlined in section F. C and G are linked, and D and H are also linked.

Reports from everyone that information was gathered from will also be included as part of the EHCNA and will be included as part of section K. These should be checked to ensure that they are all there, as this is the evidence that the EHC plan will be drafted upon, and if anything is missing, then an area of need could be missed.

The plan is reviewed at least once a year. This is a formal review of the plan, and will be carried out by the SENCo, parent and child, and a representative from the LA will be invited to attend (however, the LA rarely attend, and receive the updated plan from the school after the review meeting instead). If there are other professionals involved with supporting your pupil, they will also be invited to attend the review. At the end of the review, the plan will either: remain the same, changes will be made to parts of the plan, or the plan could be ended. Progress towards the targets will be reviewed regularly and may be each half term or term.

Most plans will stay in place until the pupil leaves education; however, the LA could decide that the pupil no longer needs the plan, in which case the plan would end. This may happen after a review meeting if it was concluded that the pupil no longer needed the plan in place. If a pupil moves home and this involves a move across to another LA, then the plan would move across with them and be transferred to the new LA.

Once the LA has decided to issue an EHC plan, then a draft version of the plan is sent to the parents. From then, there are fifteen days for the following to happen:

- Ask for changes to or make comments (officially called 'making representations') about the plan.
- For parents to give a preference of school to be named in section I of the plan.
- Ask the local authority to arrange a meeting with you to discuss the draft plan.

After this point, the LA will then:

- issue a final plan with all or some of the changes that the parents have requested;
- issue an unchanged final plan;
- make changes of their own and reissue the plan in a draft form.

If the pupil's parents are then unhappy with the plan, then there is the right to mediation and to appeal.

What is a Needs Assessment?

An Education, Health and Care Needs Assessment (EHCNA/EHC needs assessment) is the assessment that is carried out by the LA to decide whether the pupil needs to have an EHC plan. It is a legal process to be followed.

The first stage is for a request to be submitted for an EHC needs assessment to take place. This can be submitted by any of the people listed in the earlier section. There will be a great deal of evidence and information submitted for the request for an EHC needs assessment, and what will be in this, will be discussed in the upcoming sections.

The LA must carry out an EHC needs assessment if they are of the opinion that both:

- the pupil has or may have a special education need;
- the pupil may need special educational provision to be made through an EHC plan.

This is a legal threshold, which the LA must follow in making its decision whether to assess the pupil. The LA can have their own guidance or checklist to help them decide when to carry out an assessment, but the decision should always be made on an individual basis.

The LA will want to see evidence that the pupil needs more support for their special educational needs than a mainstream education setting can normally provide. It will want to see evidence of the following:

- What sort of special educational need that the pupil has or may have. This does not require a medical diagnosis.
- The amount and type of help that pupil may need, and why the school may not be able to provide this from their own resources.

The LA must inform the parents in writing within six weeks whether they are going to proceed or not with an EHC needs assessment. If the LA refuses to carry out an assessment, this could be due to them thinking that the pupil can receive all the support that they need from their current education provider, without any further additional support. Or, it could be because not enough evidence has been provided to demonstrate that your pupil needs this additional support. Parents can appeal this decision.

Once an application for an EHC needs assessment has been submitted, the LA will review the information and decide whether to proceed with an assessment.

If the LA proceed, it will gather further information about the pupil during the assessment period. This information will include the following:

- Information on parental perspectives.
- Reports from the school.
- An Educational Psychologist (EP) will carry out an assessment (even if one has already taken place and the report was submitted with the application).
- Reports from a specialist teacher if the pupil has one working with them.
- Health and social services.

- For pupils aged about 14 years, then information from advice services for preparation for adulthood.

This information is gathered within a six-week period. Once the assessment has been carried out, the LA will decide whether to issue an EHC plan or not. First, a draft plan will be sent, as outlined above, and then a final plan must be sent within a maximum of 20 weeks of the original request of an EHC needs assessment. However, services and LAs are stretched, and there are cases where this is not happening.

An outline of the timeline for an EHC needs assessment and plan is in Figure 9.1.

Weeks	Local Authority action
0	The EHC needs assessment application is submitted to the LA.
1-6	The LA processes the application. Within 6 weeks of making the request, the parents will receive a letter from your LA with a decision about the request for an EHC needs assessment. If the EHCP needs assessment is submitted and accepted, the LA will seek information from parents and professionals.
6-12	Those who are contacted for information related to the EHC needs assessment, have 6 weeks to respond. This is a legal requirement. The LA should decide whether or not to issue an EHC Plan and reach this decision by week 12. By week 12 the LA should decide if it will be able to start drafting the EHCP.
13-16	If by week 12, the LA has decided to issue an EHC Plan then it must issue the draft version by week 14, sending a copy to parents and all those who contributed to the EHC needs assessment. The parents have 15 days in which to respond to the draft with their comments and changes and to name the preferred school. Once the LA has received the parents' decision about the school placement, then they must consult with the school specified by the parents, and the school must respond with its decision within 15 days.
17-20	Between week 17 and week 20 the LA should issue the final EHCP. A copy should be sent to the parents and to the school named in the EHCP, where the pupil will be attending.
Beyond 20 weeks	The 20-week deadline is a legal deadline and any extension beyond the 20 weeks is limited to specific exceptions. The 20-week process is the maximum amount of time and the regulations say that decisions must be made as soon as is practicable, so sooner where possible.

Figure 9.1 A timeline of the EHC plan process from application for an assessment to the issuing of the plan.

Activity

Ask your SENCo whether they are currently working on putting together an EHC needs assessment, often there are on-going assessments being collated and in process. Ask the SENCo if you can shadow them, or if they can work through one of the assessments with you, so that you can see the type and amount of information that is being collated. Discuss with the SENCo what they think the strengths and weaknesses of the application may be.

The Role of the Local Authority (LA)

Let's look at the role of the LA in relation to EHC plans in further detail.

The LA has a legal duty and responsibility to identify and assess the special educational needs of pupils who are within their area. The LA must consider how best to support the pupil so that they can achieve the best outcome.

Once an EHC needs assessment has been submitted to the LA, they are then aware that a pupil may have SEN, and therefore must progress to reviewing this information as a legal requirement. If an EHC plan is issued, then the LA has a legal duty to provide what has been outlined within the plan.

The LA must publish on their website something called the 'Local Offer'. This is a comprehensive list of all the support services that it expects will be available to pupils and their families. It must include what is available locally, and what is available outside of the local area but can be accessed by those pupils and families within the LA. It should be more than just a directory of services, it should outline what is expected from the service, such as:

- what schools, colleges and other settings will provide from the funding they receive for SEN;
- what schools, colleges and other settings in its area will provide from the funding they receive to support those with a disability;
- educational, health and care provision;
- training provision;
- transport arrangements between home and school, college or early years settings;
- support for preparing for adulthood and independent living.

The Local Offer is something that is not legally binding, and the LA does not guarantee that all services will be available. However, LAs must:

- publish and maintain a clear, accessible local offer of services to support pupils with SEN and disabilities and their families;
- keep education and care provision under review and consider if it is sufficient to meet the needs of pupils in their area;
- involve parents and pupils in reviewing and developing provision for those with SEND;
- provide impartial information, advice and support on SEN and disability to parents and pupils;
- produce an EHC plan for all pupils who are assessed as needing one in a timely and inclusive manner;
- provide pupils with the support agreed in the EHC plan and review those plans annually;
- work with partner clinical commissioning groups (CCGs) to jointly commission services for pupils with SEND in their local area.

Activity

Look up the 'Local Offer' for your own Local Authority.

- What sort of services can they provide?
- How would a parent or school access these services?
- What services are part of the LA geographical area, and what are out of area?
- Why do you think this is?

EHC plans must not stop because a pupil reaches the age of 19 years. Some may need longer in education to achieve targets and outcomes. In contrast, some EHC plans will not need to stay in place until the age of 25 years.

Finally, LAs must provide Information, Advice and Support Services (IASS) to parents of SEN pupils, and this service must be provided free, be impartial and be confidential. Sometimes this service is run by a local charity rather than the LA themselves, and for other LAs, they run this service themselves.

How is funding allocated for an EHC plan?

There are three levels of funding. I will lay this out in its simplest terms as it can get complex, there can be disputes over how funding is spent, and funding changes.

Level 1:

This is money that is given by the government to every school for every child. It does not matter whether a child has SEND or not, the funding is given to the school per the number of pupils on roll. This money should cover the cost of staffing and premises.

Level 2:

This funding is allocated for each pupil that needs SEN support. It is (at the time of writing this book) £6000 per child. It is known as the Notional SEN budget. It is up to the school how to use this money, some schools will use it on staffing support, training or resources.

Level 3:

This is known as the High Needs Block or top-up funding, which is paid by the Local Authority or the Education and Skills Funding Agency. This is money allocated to meet the needs of an EHC plan. Depending upon the level of the EHC plan and the pupil's individual needs, then this amount can vary from several hundred pounds to many thousands of pounds depending on whether a pupil needs a specialist or residential placement.

High needs block funding is given in levels, and recently has changed from numbered levels to lettered levels. Figure 9.2 shows an example which replicates what LAs might outline, as the level of need associated with each banding level, and then a funding allocation is given to each of these banding levels by the LA.

Banding Level	Banding Descriptor
Band A	Pupils at this level make slower than expected progress or give some other cause for concern. Needs can be met by targeted adaptive teaching and highly focused lesson design and modifying programmes of work. A pupil requiring this level of support will experience difficulties for which a mainstream school can address with support from within the graduated approach. Outside agencies will be involved if school-based interventions are not leading to the desired outcomes, and further specialist expertise may be needed, for example, Occupational Therapy, CAMHS, SLT, EP, and Specialist Teachers.
Band B	Pupils at this level can have their needs met in mainstream classes, predominantly working on modified curriculum tasks. This should include drawing on the specialist advice of services, or direct support by LA services and other agencies, as appropriate. The graduated approach has been implemented and will have included interventions recommended by outside agencies, but progress is not meeting the desired outcomes. In order to achieve the desired outcomes for the pupil, the school needs to access resources beyond that of the school through an Educational Health Care Plan. The EHC plan will support the school to provide opportunities for small group work based on identified need with opportunities for one-to-one support.
Band C	Pupils in this band will have an EHC plan. Pupils requiring this level of support will continue to make slower progress than expected and experience a moderate level of difficulties or a combination of moderate difficulties as outlined in Part II of this book. Pupils at this level will have attainments well below expected levels in all or most areas of the curriculum, despite appropriate interventions. They have much greater difficulty than their peers in acquiring basic literacy and numeracy skills and in understanding concepts. They may also have associated speech and language delay, low self-esteem, low levels of concentration and underdeveloped social skills. Pupils within this band may be described as having moderate learning difficulties (MLD) or global, general or generalised learning difficulties.
Band D	Pupils in this band will have an EHC plan. Pupils will have substantial and/or significant difficulty in accessing the curriculum because of their identified needs. Pupils at this level may have attainments well below expected levels in some or all areas of the curriculum, despite appropriate interventions. They may have much greater difficulty than their peers in acquiring basic literacy and numeracy skills and will have greater difficulties than their peers in understanding concepts. They may also have associated speech and language delay disorder, low self-esteem, low levels of concentration and underdeveloped social skills. Pupils within this band may be described as having moderate learning difficulties (MLD) or global, general or generalised learning difficulties.
Band E	Pupils in this band will have an EHC plan. It is expected that pupils requiring this level of support will experience a combination of substantial or severe difficulty in the areas of communication, cognitive development, behaviour, emotional well-being, physical difficulty and/or sensory impairment. They are likely to have significant cognitive impairments. They may also have associated difficulties in mobility and acquisition of self-help skills. All pupils requiring this level of support will require specialist provision. Pupils within this band may have severe learning difficulties (SLD).

Banding Level	Banding Descriptor
Band F	Pupils in this band will have an EHC plan. Pupils requiring support at this level will have a combination of substantial and severe difficulties in areas of communication, cognitive development, behaviour, emotional well-being, physical difficulty, or sensory impairment which significantly impacts on all areas of functioning both within and outside school. They are likely to have significant cognitive impairments. They may also have associated difficulties in mobility and acquisition of self-help skills. All children requiring this level of support will require specialist provision. Pupils within this band may have severe learning difficulties (SLD). Most of these children will be educated within a specialist provision.
Band G	Pupils in this band will have an EHC plan. Band G level of support is for those pupils with special educational needs likely to be met by a highly specialist setting able to deal with profound and complex permanent needs. These are likely to arise from a combination of medical, primary care, learning, and communication, behavioural, physical, and sensory needs (including multi-sensory impairment). All pupils requiring support at this level will meet the requirements for specialist provision. Pupils will also have exceptional needs in the areas of behaviour, physical, medical or communication needs. For pupils requiring Band G level of support when behaviour is a concern this will be extremely challenging for experienced and suitably trained staff. Where medical or physical needs are a particular concern, constant or a high-level of monitoring and medical intervention will be required throughout the day. They are also likely to require full time adult support to access all learning. Positive behaviour plans will require targeted and planned support from more than one adult for most of the day. Where communication is a concern, the pupil will rely on a trained adult to access a communication tool to communicate basic needs. Pupils who require Band G level of support may be described as having profound and multiple learning difficulties (PMLD). They are at a very early stage of development and need people around them who can help them to explore and interpret the world.

Figure 9.2 An example of a summary of needs for EHC plan banding.

The Parental Role in Applying for an EHC Plan

A parent can apply for an EHC needs assessment, and they do not need a school to apply on their behalf or need the support of the school. However, a school would need to provide supporting evidence towards the pupil needing to have provision above what they can provide as a school, so the LA would contact the school for the relevant information as part of their assessment. Often, it is the school that applies for the EHC needs assessment with the support of the parents.

The parents will be asked to provide supporting documentation which could include any medical reports previously received, reports from professionals, or additional services that they have used. They will be asked to provide their concerns, and thoughts around the provision needed for their child, and they will be asked to complete a questionnaire.

Once the application for an EHC needs assessment has been submitted, the correspondence will come to them as the parent. They will be advised whether an assessment will be taking place, and they will be notified of any key points and a timeline along the way.

The parents will need to review a draft plan, and to seek support and advice on this if it is needed. They can ask for elements of the plan to be amended, and if they do not agree to the final plan, then they can seek mediation or progress to an appeal. Parents will also list their preferred school for their child on the plan. It is not guaranteed that the LA will be able to agree this school; the school will need to agree that they can meet the needs of the pupil with the provision that has been outlined in the plan, and some schools such as special schools will be heavily oversubscribed and will not have the capacity to take another pupil. In this case, alternative suitable schools should be offered by the LA.

Once a pupil is at school with their EHC plan, then parents will attend review meetings to discuss their child's progress with the class teacher and with the SENCo at the annual review meeting. It is important that communication is open and transparent between parents and school staff; at times supporting a SEN pupil can be challenging, and relationships can break down between the schools and parents. Keep discussions open and regular, review meetings should not be the only time that contact is made with the parents.

The Role of the SENCo - Applying for an EHC Needs Assessment, Implementing and Reviewing the EHC Plan

Application for an EHC needs assessment

The SENCo will decide in discussion with the class teacher and with pupil's parents that the pupil needs support beyond what is available, and what can be given with the current level of funding in school. As mentioned earlier, anyone can apply for an EHC needs assessment, but most commonly it is the pupil's educational setting such as the school, sometimes it is a parent, and occasionally it is another service or adult such as a family member. For this section, we are going to look at a school perspective.

A decision to apply for an EHC needs assessment may be on-going for several months or even years. Evidence needs to be gathered over a period of time, and deciding when the school can no longer meet a pupil's needs, and when they will need further support, can be a tricky moment to judge, and sometimes all parties (the school and parents) may not agree on this timing. Either way, a range of evidence will be needed by a range of professionals. This evidence may include:

- the level of academic attainment, and the rate of progress that is being made by the pupil;
- the nature, extent, and context of their needs;
- the interventions that have been put into place by the school already;
- evidence of physical, emotional and social needs;
- evidence of working with external professionals, that their advice has been implemented and reviewed. For example, from an Educational Psychologist (EP), Speech and Language Therapist (SLT) and/or specialist teacher;

- that additional support and provision has been implemented beyond the SEN level of support expected by a school;
- that the request for additional provision will support the pupil to make increased progress;
- several cycles of the assess-plan-do-review cycle as outlined in the graduated approach in Chapter 8 have taken place.

The SENCo will submit all of this information with a completed form to the LA, and the parents will be asked for their views to accompany this request. There is still no guarantee a progression to an assessment will take place.

Implementing and reviewing an EHC plan

When the needs assessment has taken place, and if successful, and the EHC plan has been issued, what next?

The parents will name a preferred school on the plan, and the LA will approach the school to see if they are able to meet the needs of the pupil with the additional support in place through the EHC plan. A school can either say yes, no, or negotiate what they may need to support the pupil. Once a school has been agreed, then the plan will be put into place through the school, with the support of the LA. For example, what resources the school will provide, what external expertise is needed, and what funding is needed will be discussed. The legal responsibility of the implementation of the plan remains with the LA.

The school then decides how to use the provision based on what is in the EHC plan and what is outlined in section F of the plan, and how specifically this is outlined. This may include direct and indirect work with a pupil.

The plan is reviewed annually, as mentioned earlier, but progress and targets will be reviewed more regularly. The SENCo will lead the review, and may or may not lead the interim review points. Once the annual review has taken place, then the SENCo will send off the updated plan to the LA to approve this.

The Role of the Teacher - Applying for an EHC Needs Assessment, Implementing and Reviewing the EHC Plan

Application for an EHC needs assessment

The class teacher will support the SENCo when they gather their evidence ready to make an application for an EHC needs assessment. Robust recording of information throughout the graduated approach assess-plan-do-review cycles are needed. There should be at least two cycles of this, but often there may be more, which may span more than a year. It is vital that the recording and storing of this information is well organised so that it can be retrieved, reviewed and collated when it is needed.

Your SENCo will call on you for data for the pupil, evidence of the implementation of additional support and interventions, and the impact of these. This evidence will also be drawn from Individual Education Plans (IEPs) and the reviews from these, which you may have led on as the class teacher.

The SENCo may also ask you to complete further check lists and questionnaires relating to your pupil, and you may also need to complete some of these with your pupil from their perspective.

Implementing and reviewing an EHC plan

Once an EHC plan has been issued for your pupil, the SENCo will work with you to look at the provision and support that has been set out in section F of the plan, and decide what this looks like in real terms within the classroom, or for the additional provision. You will work with the SENCo to implement this provision.

The review of the plan has been outlined, and you will participate in this review by providing your perspective on the progress being made towards the outcomes. This will then become an on-going cycle for pupils with EHC plans that come in and out of your classes as they move up the year groups.

CASE STUDY

Johan is a trainee teacher.

Johan was in term two of his teacher training course and was undertaking a 50% teaching block practice. Archie was a pupil in Johan's class. Archie had received a diagnosis of Autism, the previous year. He also had dyslexia indicators and general anxiety disorder, which could impact upon his attendance at school.

Archie had coped well in primary school so far, with the additional support that was in place, and because it was a large primary school, there was a substantial range of intervention programmes being implemented which Archie could join. These included:

- Anxiety support group/nurture group.
- One-to-one time with the school support dog, talking with him about feelings, and taking responsibility and care for another being.
- Social skills development group once a week.
- Playground support group, daily (or Lego therapy).
- Lego therapy (on days when not in the playground).
- Read, Write, Inc phonics programme, twice a week.
- Narrative group programme (alternating with the Language support programme half termly, once a week).
- Language support programme.

(Continued)

The school were meeting his needs by going above and beyond what would normally be expected.

Archie's parents were becoming increasingly concerned as the end of primary school was beginning to approach, by what the future held for Archie and his transition to secondary school. They were worried about how he would cope in such a large busy environment, without the sort of level of support that he was currently receiving from his primary school. The SENCo and parents met and agreed that it would be timely to consider putting in an application for an EHC needs assessment, in preparation for Archie's transition to a secondary school, so that the additional support that they felt would be needed, could be planned for.

The class teacher had been implementing Archie's IEP and had reviewed his targets at the end of term one. Targets for term two were being worked upon as part of the information gathering and assess-plan-do-review cycle. Johan had observed the review meeting at the end of term one, and the next review meeting was due to take place. Johan worked with his class teacher (and mentor) to gather the evidence to demonstrate what progress Archie was making towards the targets, and what areas were still areas of difficulty for him. These included aspects of literacy, which Archie was attending interventions for, and challenges around Archie's Social, Emotional and Mental Health (SEMH) linked to his anxiety and sensory needs. Johan discussed Archie's progress with the LSAs that were leading the support group sessions. Johan was asked to lead on aspects of the review meeting as he had a good understanding of Archie's classroom and academic progress as he had been teaching 50% of the time.

As Johan progressed into term three of his teacher training, he was invited to join the SENCo and class teacher in collating and formulating the application for the EHC needs assessment. Johan stated 'this has been an extremely helpful experience for me during my teacher training, I have a much better understanding of the amount of work needed to apply for an EHC needs assessment, and how my role as the class teacher is instrumental in this. I will ensure that my information gathering and recording is tight as this could impact upon an application!'

PROFESSIONAL **DISCUSSION**

Arrange a meeting with your mentor to discuss EHC needs assessments and EHC plans.

- What has been their recent experience and role within applying for an EHC needs assessment for one of their pupils?
- What did they do, and how did this form a part of the graduated approach outlined in Chapter 8?

Chapter Summary

This chapter has outlined what an Education, Health and Care (EHC) plan is, what it looks like, and how it is reviewed. It has discussed that an Education, Health and Care (EHC) needs assessment happens first, before an EHC plan can be issued, and outlined the process and information needed for this to happen.

The role of the Local Authority (LA) has been explored, and the underpinning factor that the LA has a legal responsibility with the assessment of SEN pupils, and the issuing and implementation of an EHC plan.

Both the role of the SENCo and the class teacher within the application process, the implementation of an EHC plan, and the review of it has been set out.

Glossary of Key Terms

- Information, Advice and Support Services (IASS) – A service for parents of SEN pupils run by the LA. This service is provided free, it is impartial, and it is confidential.
- Education and Health Care Needs Assessment (EHC needs assessment/ EHCNA) – An assessment undertaken by the Local Authority (LA) to decide whether an EHC plan should be issued.
- Education and Health Care Plan (EHC plan) – A legal document for children and young people aged up to the age of 25 years who need more support than is available through special educational needs support.

Further Reading

- Gov.UK Children with Special Educational Needs and Disabilities. https://www.gov.uk/children-with-special-educational-needs/extra-SEN-help
- Independent Advisor of Special Education Advice (IPSEA). https://www.ipsea.org.uk/pages/category/education-health-and-care-plans

Links to the Teachers' Standards

- *2. Promote good progress and outcomes by pupils;* be accountable for pupils' attainment, progress and outcomes; be aware of pupils' capabilities and their prior knowledge, and plan teaching to build on these; guide pupils to reflect on the progress they have made and their emerging needs

- *5. Adapt teaching to respond to the strengths and needs of all pupils*; have a secure understanding of how a range of factors can inhibit pupils' ability to learn, and how best to overcome these; have a clear understanding of the needs of all pupils, including those with special educational needs; those of high ability; those with English as an additional language; those with disabilities; and be able to use and evaluate distinctive teaching approaches to engage and support them.
- *8. Fulfil wider professional responsibilities;* develop effective professional relationships with colleagues, knowing how and when to draw on advice and specialist support, communicate effectively with parents with regard to pupils' achievements and well-being.

References

Contact for families with disabled children. https://contact.org.uk/help-for-families/information-advice-services/education-start/education-learning/ehc-plans-assessments/getting-an-ehc-draft-plan/

Conclusion

The Future of SEND

Chapter Aims

- To review the progress made in SEND developments within schools.
- To consider the future of new policy and practice to support pupils in primary schools.
- To forward plan for the next steps as an Early Career Teacher (ECT) and working with SEND pupils.

Links to the Core Content Framework (CCF)

Adaptive Teaching

- ***Learn that*** seeking to understand pupils' differences, including their different levels of prior knowledge and potential barriers to learning, is an essential part of teaching.
- ***Learn that*** pupils with special educational needs or disabilities are likely to require additional or adapted support; working closely with colleagues, families and pupils to understand barriers and identify effective strategies is essential.
- ***Learn how to*** receive clear, consistent and effective mentoring in supporting pupils with a range of additional needs, including how to use the SEND Code of Practice, which provides additional guidance on supporting pupils with SEND effectively.

Links to the Early Career Framework (ECF)

Adaptive Teaching

- ***Learn that*** seeking to understand pupils' differences, including their different levels of prior knowledge and potential barriers to learning, is an essential part of teaching.
- ***Learn that*** pupils with special educational needs or disabilities are likely to require additional or adapted support; working closely with colleagues, families and pupils to understand barriers and identify effective strategies is essential.
- ***Learn how to*** work closely with the Special Educational Needs Co-ordinator (SENCo) and special education professionals and the Designated Safeguarding Lead.
- ***Learn how to*** use the SEND Code of Practice, which provides additional guidance on supporting pupils with SEND effectively.

Introduction

As you near the end of your teacher training, this chapter begins by introducing not only the relevant sections of your entitlement of the Core Content Framework (CCF), but also the relevant sections of the Early Career Framework (ECF) which you will be moving into during your ECT years.

These short conclusions are going to review the progress that has been made with SEND developments in school in this ever-changing landscape. Then it will consider the future of the policy and new developments that are being proposed. Finally, the chapter will consider your own next steps when working with SEND pupils as you move into your ECT years.

The Progress Made in SEND Developments in School

Over a decade ago, Brian Lamb conducted an inquiry and stated that there needed to be a radical overhaul of the SEND system. But how far have we come? Has there been greater ambition for SEND pupils?

We have had the introduction of the SEND Code of Practice (2015), but Ofsted (2021a) concluded that some Local Authorities (LAs) and schools have struggled to implement the reforms, and were not implementing the legal requirements that have been set out, with a lack of co-production and poor-quality EHC plans, issues with the identification and assessment of pupils with SEND and confusion over who is accountable for what.

There are other issues relating to the lack of ambition for SEND pupils, with attendance being below average, and employment figures after education very low. Ofsted (2021b) also argue that there are unmet needs of SEND pupils in schools, where basic skills have not been identified or mastered yet by pupils.

Ofsted declare that there is still much to do, such as strengthening the quality of the curriculum, and providing high quality teaching for all.

Schools are busy places, but our SEND pupils deserve to get the best quality teaching and support that they can. This book aims to give you a much better understanding of SEND systems, supports, and strategies so that as a developing trainee teacher, you are better prepared to support your SEND pupils with the knowledge that you have gained.

The Future of New Policy and Practice to Support Pupils in Primary Schools

The SEND and Alternative Provision (AP) Improvement Plan

Where are we at now? As you will recall from right back to the beginning of this book, in Chapter 1, a green paper was published as part of a consultation around SEND provision in schools, then from this, the SEND and AP Improvement Plan (2023) was created and published, setting out the government's proposals to improve outcomes for pupils through:

- improving experiences for families, reducing the current adversity and frustration that they face;
- delivering financial sustainability of the system;
- relieving pressure on the current AP sector.

They are aiming to deliver this through their mission:

- Fulfil children's potential: children and young people with SEND (or attending alternative provision) enjoy their childhood, achieve good outcomes and are well prepared for adulthood and employment.

- Build parents' trust: parents and carers experience a fairer, easily navigable system (across education, health and care) that restores their confidence that their children will get the right support, in the right place, at the right time.
- Provide financial sustainability: local leaders make the best use of record investment in the high needs budget to meet children and young people's needs and improve outcomes, while placing local authorities on a stable financial footing.

DfE (2023)

We still have a long way to go with the implementation of these proposals, and things can change quickly in government, with each new Secretary for Education wanting to put their own mark on education. It is therefore important to keep up to date with any changes, and what these mean for you and your SEND pupils, and we will all continue to do our best for them.

Next Steps as an Early Career Teacher (ECT) and Working with SEND Pupils

Early Career Framework and SEND

As you know, the Early Career Framework builds upon the Core Content Framework, and it is clear to see the similarities in the frameworks. Review both of the frameworks and identify the strands that relate directly to working with SEND pupils.

By reviewing the frameworks, you will see, for example, the CCF Adaptive Teaching Standard 5, learn how to statement reads:

Provide opportunity for all pupils to experience success, by:

- Observing how expert colleagues adapt lessons, whilst maintaining high expectations for all, so that all pupils have the opportunity to meet expectations and deconstructing this approach.
- Discussing and analysing with expert colleagues how to balance input of new content so that pupils master important concepts.

And – following expert input – by taking opportunities to practise, receive feedback and improve at:

- Making effective use of teaching assistants and other adults in the classroom under supervision of expert colleagues.

Whereas the ECF Adaptive Teaching Standard 5, learn how to statement reads:

Provide opportunity for all pupils to experience success, by:

- Adapting lessons, whilst maintaining high expectations for all, so that all pupils have the opportunity to meet expectations.
- Balancing input of new content so that pupils master important concepts.
- Making effective use of teaching assistants.

With the difference in your own role of being supervised, discussing, and analysing, to now being responsible for these elements, and in turn the impact on your pupils.

Reflect

Which areas of the CCF that relates to SEND pupils do you feel as though you have had a good deal of opportunity to learn about and put into practice?

Which areas may you want to gain further experience of still?

When you look at the same areas within the ECF, how do these change?

In terms of your responsibilities as a teacher, which areas will you need further support with when you move to your ECT years? How can they be formulated into targets or opportunities?

Begin to draft these potential targets, or list opportunities you would like to take in your forthcoming year, so that you can take these to your first meeting with your ECT mentor. It is ok to identify areas of practice and experience that you still need to develop, this is what your time as an ECT is for.

Recap of the Book

This book was split into three parts:

- The first part looked at policy development and the professional roles and responsibilities of educational professionals, and yourself as a teacher when working with SEND pupils.
- The second part focused on the four broad areas of need as outlined within the SEND Code of Practice, looking at examples of the need and strategies to support pupils with this need.
- The third and final part of the book looked at developing classroom practice, including working with support staff and other educational professionals, gaining an understanding of high quality teaching and assessing pupil need through the graduated approach, and developing your understanding of the Education, Health and Care Plan.

Final Words

As you continue on your teaching journey and career, reflect on how far you have developed over your training course. The learning that you have undertaken has been vast. As you move forward, you will continue to learn and develop, and your knowledge and skills when working with your SEND and neurodivergent pupils will develop too.

Stay on top of the changing landscape in Education and SEND, and be ready to make changes. Aim to become an expert, and to make a difference to the pupils in your care that need you to support them to achieve their best and go on to lead fulfilling lives. You can make a difference to each and every one that progresses through your classes. Best of luck with your Career in Education!

Further Reading

- Department for Education (2019). Early Career Framework. https://assets.publishing.service.gov.uk/government/uploads/system/uploads/attachment_data/file/978358/Early-Career_Framework_April_2021.pdf
- Department for Education (DfE) (2023). SEND and Alternative Provision Improvement Plan. https://www.gov.uk/government/publications/send-and-alternative-provision-improvement-plan
- Department for Education (DfE) (2023). SEND and Alternative Provision Improvement Plan Roadmap. https://www.gov.uk/government/publications/send-and-alternative-provision-improvement-plan/send-and-alternative-provision-roadmap

Links to the Teachers' Standards

- *8. Fulfil wider professional responsibilities*; take responsibility for improving teaching through appropriate professional development, responding to advice and feedback from colleagues.

PART TWO: PERSONAL AND PROFESSIONAL CONDUCT

- 3 Teachers must have an understanding of, and always act within, the statutory frameworks which set out their professional duties and responsibilities.

References

Department for Education (DfE) (2015). Special Educational Needs and Disabilities Code of Practice; 0 to 25 Years. DfE.

Department for Education (2019). Early Career Framework. https://assets.publishing.service.gov.uk/government/uploads/system/uploads/attachment_data/file/978358/Early-Career_Framework_April_2021.pdf

Department for Education (DfE) (2023). SEND and Alternative Provision Improvement Plan. https://www.gov.uk/government/publications/send-and-alternative-provision-improvement-plan

Department for Education (DfE) (2023). SEND and Alternative Provision Improvement Plan Roadmap. https://www.gov.uk/government/publications/send-and-alternative-provision-improvement-plan/send-and-alternative-provision-roadmap

Gov.UK and Ofsted (2021a). SEND: Old Issues, New Issues, Next Steps. https://www.gov.uk/government/publications/send-old-issues-new-issues-next-steps/send-old-issues-new-issues-next-steps

Gov.UK and Ofsted (2021b). Supporting SEND. https://www.gov.uk/government/publications/supporting-send/supporting-send

Index

Zeitfracht Medien GmbH
Ferdinand-Jühlke-Straße 7
99095 Erfurt, Deutschland
produktsicherheit@kolibri360.de